The Genius of
JAMES BARBER

The Genius of JAMES BARBER

His Best Recipes

HARBOUR PUBLISHING

Harbour Publishing Co. Ltd
P.O. Box 219, Madeira Park, BC, V0N2H0
www.harbourpublishing.com

Edited by Sarah Weber
Indexed by Hugh Morrison
Photographs courtesy Christina Burridge
    and the estate of James Barber
Text design and layout by Five Seventeen, Picapica.ca
Text illustrations by James Barber and Kim Lafave
Cover illustration by Kim Lafave
Cover design by Anna Comfort

Printed in Canada

Harbour Publishing acknowledges financial support from
the Government of Canada through the Book Publishing
Industry Development Program and the Canada Council for
the Arts, and from the Province of British Columbia through
the BC Arts Council and the Book Publishing Tax Credit.

Canada Council   Conseil des Arts
for the Arts   du Canada

BRITISH
COLUMBIA
ARTS COUNCIL
Supported by the Province of British Columbia

LIBRARY AND ARCHIVES CANADA CATALOGUING IN PUBLICATION

Barber, James, 1923–2007.
    The genius of James Barber : his best recipes.

Includes index.
ISBN 978-1-55017-449-6

    1. Cookery. 2. Barber, James, 1923-2007. I. Title.

TX714.B3648 2008   641.5   C2008-905916-6

Printed on paper containing 30% post consumer waste

In memory of James.

CONTENTS

Preface

ANGELA MURRILLS

FOOD AND RESTAURANT COLUMNIST AND AUTHOR

Any time any one of us throws together supper from what's in the pantry, or realizes we're out of white wine but it's okay to use apple juice instead, or takes any other kind of first step out on a culinary limb, we owe a nod to James Barber. Forget the Barber bit. As far as most people were concerned, he was simply "James," a splendid cook—he was far too down-to-earth to ever call himself a chef—and a wonderful writer. Ingredients, words … he treated them the same, so that what came out of his oven or his typewriter (and later his laptop) was simplicity, honesty, abundant flavour and, for the eater or reader, a deep sense of satisfaction.

These days, we're awash with foodie blogs, foodie websites, foodie magazines and FoodTV, but it wasn't always like that, and it's important to remember that James was way ahead of the game. But let's back up a bit to his pre-cooking career. British-born, he had played his part in World War II, leading a small squad behind enemy lines in France where—the start of his peasant leanings—he learned to live off the land. Emigrating to Canada in 1952, he brought with him expertise in physics, surveying and engineering, which got him work on major backcountry projects in British Columbia, his home for more than fifty years.

All the while, he cooked. Not in shiny professional kitchens but on small boats and in logging camps. Then, sidelined by a skiing accident in the 1960s, he started writing book reviews, then theatre reviews, and ultimately got into writing about food. He did other things too: acting, swapping shirts with Mick Jagger and, in 1971, publishing his first cookbook.

Like many, I first "met" James through his recipes when, in 1980, new to Vancouver, I picked up an odd-shaped little book called *Fear of Frying*. Soon I was making my way through African chicken and "Immanuel Kant's two pork chops, some celery and two big old carrots recipe." This was the yuppie era, remember—a best-forgotten time of pretentious plates and confusion cuisine. James was never one for tarting up food and, while most '80s cookbooks now look plain silly (did chefs really weave strips of salmon and spinach leaves into poachable "mats"?), his are still bang up-to-date and still very alluring. Read his recipes and you want to go putter in the kitchen. And that was his aim.

"My cookbooks," he wrote, "are blatant attempts to seduce, to encourage people to experiment and

Corporal Barber, c.1941 in the Royal Air Force, prior to going behind enemy lines in Europe and learning to cook with the peasants.

wander up the sideroads of their imagination." He did the same through his restaurant reviews. Thirty years ago, Vancouver had only a handful of eateries but, as more opened and as the years went by, he introduced readers to all of them. Not just the posh expense-account places but also the little mom-and-pop holes in the wall that dished up fantastic noodles. Today we all know our way around ethnic menus, but we didn't back then. He was the guide who took us there, the trailblazer, the teacher. (James taught me how to review restaurants: "If there's a patio, make sure it gets the sun"; how to make notes: afterwards, when you've left the restaurant; and how, in dire straits, to tuck the menu down your pants for later reference.)

Long before it was chic to make a fuss about local ingredients, he was wandering city laneways foraging for greens, mushrooms and whatever else he could find. One time I joined him and, as we ambled up and down the secret alleys that hide between the rear manicured gardens of the multimillion-dollar mansions in Vancouver's West Point Grey, we came upon hazelnuts, ceps and rosehips. You can make tea from rosehips, he said. He knew a lot, that man.

Years before the term "comfort food" became trendy, James was coaxing us to cook lamb shanks and risotto Milanese: "a care and nurturing recipe. A *kind* dinner." Kindness was central to his cooking and his life. *His* secret side was that he taught cooking to new immigrants, to school kids and to people without a penny to bless themselves.

As the host of *The Urban Peasant*, his face became known worldwide (he was especially pleased to be dubbed in Tagalog). These days, celebrity chefs abound, but James was the first to make cooking look fun and easy. Rustling up dinner isn't hard if you have time and money galore, but he showed you how to cook something quick and tasty with what you already had in the kitchen or could pick up at the supermarket. And what a prophetic title

On the Nechako River near Kemano, BC in the early '50s—James always loved fishing.

The Urban Peasant turned out to be. Today, as we water our heirloom tomato plants, plant communal gardens and browse farmers' markets, aren't we all striving for urban peasanthood?

The talents of this lovely man extended far and wide. James wrote opera reviews and enchanting poems for kids (all kids loved him). He was a master of comic verse who was thrilled that, only the week before he left us, *The Tyee* (www.thetyee.ca) published a sharp bit of political satire, yet another string he planned to add to his bow. He was also, as those first little cookbooks show, a whimsical cartoonist, not to mention a competent pruner of vines, guitarist, bocce player and tractor driver around his property on Vancouver Island. His sense of humour was Rabelaisian to the point that I cannot include even one of the many jokes he told me (but I can still hear his mischievous growly chuckle). Nor can I read a fortune-cookie fortune without remembering his advice to always tack "in bed" to the end of it. Try it.

Even more than making people laugh, James loved feeding them. At Expo 86, I watched him speedily make a dish of chicken wings and rice large enough to satisfy thirty. You could see the crowd's thought bubble: "If he can do that, we can too." And they probably went home and did. For many years, he and his wife, Christina Burridge, hosted a Bastille Day party centred on *le grand aïoli* and a lusty communal singing of "La Marseillaise." He may have called himself a peasant, but this was a man who lived the richest possible life.

For James, cooking and love were inextricably intertwined. Cooking, he wrote, "ought to be a shared courtship, a foreplay to the intimacy of a shared dinner." The cover of what turned out to be his final cookbook wasn't the usual stylist-tweaked plate or author's photo but a pair of affectionately entwined carrots.

Fittingly, two is how many most of his recipes serve, sometimes with leftovers, often in under thirty minutes in a frying pan on top of the stove. Seasonality? He was on to that long before it became fashionable. "I teach people that in the winter you eat a lot of cabbage because it's cheap," he once wrote. Cabbage, as he pointed out, can be cooked, or cut up in a salad or made into a comfortable bed for flavourful sausages. His books included recipes for mundane vegetables like carrots and everyday fruits like oranges. "The things that people have got," James said. "It's all corner-store stuff."

He lived his last years far from corner-store country on twelve acres in Cobble Hill on Vancouver Island, where he grew potatoes, beans, arugula, lots of garlic—"six hundred heads of garlic"—and winter kale. Getting beef, pork and eggs from his neighbours, eating his own strawberries, raspberries and blueberries come summer,

building a trout pond: he loved it all with the lusty vigour that was the essence of his character, recording his adventures online (even in his eighties, he was no Luddite).

He always stressed that his recipes were not prescriptions. "This is how to cook. A lot of recipes are paint-by-numbers. This teaches you how to improvise," he said of one of his books. And to improvise together. But remember that when he stipulated two, he wrote once, "They don't have to be lovers—there's nothing more rewarding than cooking with a three-year-old, unless it's skating around the back end of an eighty-year-old gran, watching how she makes the recipe she somehow can't write down for you." He did workshops in schools. "There's only one rule in teaching kids to cook," he said to me once. "Tell them it's the best thing they've ever had in their lives. They'll eat it

The Urban Peasant charmed viewers around the globe by showing that cooking could be fun and easy.

James offers up fresh grilled sardines at Deerholme Farm, Duncan, BC, in 2007.

and they'll try anything else afterwards." (James always had the wide-eyed enthusiasm and down-right glee of a six-year-old, whether it was over a new restaurant he had discovered or the donkeys that he installed on his farm.)

The ultimate urban peasant was part of our family for more than twenty-five years. My husband, Peter, who met James during the making of the TV commercials for mmmarvellous mushrooms, which made James a household name—was so delighted by his first attempt at recreating James's Portuguese Pork and Clams (page 71) that he has cooked it regularly ever since. At age six, our daughter, Kate, appeared with James on *The Urban Peasant* and together they put together bread, butter and jam. At twenty-four, she visited James on his farm, where he showed her how to use a milk frother to make unimaginably good scrambled eggs, to roast nuts in the microwave

and "how amazing corn tastes when you rub it with fresh lime, not butter." That she, and count-less others of her generation, now cook from scratch is only a small part of the legacy he left.

Back in 1971, these were the very first words that James wrote in his cookbook *Ginger Tea Makes Friends*: "Cooking is the simplest way of saying I love you. That may sound pretentious as hell, but if you accept it as essential, your cooking will improve—and so will your love life. There is so much mystique in the kitchen, all mixed up with social acceptance, and fancy linen, and the right kind of spoons. I learned how to cook in tin mess kits in France, and now I cook on a beat-up fifty-year-old stove in a kitchen covered with books, and a typewriter on the table, or on a sail-boat at sea. I have a lot of pots and pans but mostly I use a heavy iron fry pan with a lid.

"I like candles, and I have a lot of saucers to put them on. I use a lot of herbs and I usually measure them in the palm of my hand. A tight-squeezed palm is a teaspoon, medium a dessertspoon, and a really open one a tablespoon. Measure out some spoonfuls, see how they look in your hand, then forget the spoons and start feeling your food as you cook it. That's really the secret—touch it a bit."

Over the years, James touched the hearts, minds and funny bones of hundreds of thousands of people and spurred them on to discover the deep joy of feeding themselves and the people they care about. For those of us who knew him, this book is like a chat with an old friend. If this is your first meeting with James, all I can say is I envy you. Just know that you're at the start of a long and delicious friendship.

WHAT WE ARE NOW ABOUT TO DO IS VERY GOURMET SO MAKE SURE THEY NOTICE.

BREAKFASTS

GRILLED GRAPEFRUIT

HALVE A GRAPEFRUIT. Place it on an ovenproof plate and sprinkle with some brown sugar. Broil in the toaster oven until the sugar is bubbling. Serve immediately.

MARBLED YOGURT

SPRINKLE A LITTLE BROWN SUGAR over a small bowl of yogurt and let stand, undisturbed, for a couple of hours or overnight in the fridge. The sugar will slowly melt down into the yogurt, and you'll end up with a pretty, marbled breakfast or dessert that needs nothing more than a few wedges of sliced apple arranged on it and a dusting of cinnamon.

BREAKFAST TOFU WITH MAPLE SYRUP
`2 SERVINGS`

Trust me ... just try it!

1 Tbsp [15 mL] soy sauce
1 Tbsp [15 mL] vegetable oil
1 pkg [500 g] firm tofu, cut into finger-sized strips
Maple syrup
Juice of 1 grapefruit
Pinch of cayenne pepper

HEAT THE SOY SAUCE and oil in a frying pan over high heat. Add the tofu and cook until browned on both sides. Drizzle with maple syrup, pour the grapefruit juice over top, sprinkle with just a bit of cayenne and serve.

THE PERFECT POACHED EGG

NOW THE POACHED EGG ... You can buy an egg poacher (most people seem to get them as presents at showers), which is a set of little dishes set in a base. They will indeed produce a perfectly formed poached egg, usually as hard as a hockey puck—and just as comforting as one.

But the really great poached egg (which will sit equally well on toast or a bed of mashed potatoes) requires a small to medium-sized saucepan half-filled with water, a slotted spoon, a saucer and a teaspoon [5 mL] of vinegar. Boil the water, add the vinegar and crack an egg into a saucer. This is a business of perfection, not a production line. You have to fuss, so enjoy it—one egg at a time.

Stir the water in the saucepan carefully and vigorously until it's spinning fast, with a vortex in the middle like the water going down the bathtub drain. Now slide the egg directly into the centre of the spinning water, keeping the pan on high heat. Let the egg come to rest; the yolk will be in the middle, with the white all tucked up around it. Cook the egg for 3 minutes (you don't have to time it, you'll see when it's just right) and remove it from the water with a slotted spoon. Put the egg on toast, sprinkle it with a little pepper and salt, and carry it, triumphantly, to the table (or better still the bedside) of your best beloved. Better than any valentine.

EGG IN A NEST
`1 SERVING`

Serve this egg dish with some cherry tomatoes or asparagus that has been sautéed in hot oil for a minute.

1 slice bread
1 Tbsp [15 mL] butter
1 egg
Paprika
Salt and pepper
Chopped parsley

CUT A CIRCLE out of the slice of bread with a wine glass. Fry the bread (and the circle) on one side. Turn the bread over and break the egg into the hole. Sprinkle with a little paprika and some salt and pepper, and cook until the egg white is set. Serve with the bread circle propped up against the side. Garnish with parsley.

SCRAMBLED EGGS WITH MUSHROOMS
`1 SERVING`

For breakfast, lunch or a quick supper, scrambled eggs are virtually foolproof. Everybody has a special trick, some secret handed down from a grandmother or obtained from a spouse. Some people use water, some use milk, but very few know about tarragon, that sweet, gentle herb the French use so enthusiastically with eggs and fish. Tarragon also goes very well with mushrooms. The quantities in this recipe are for one person, because I always seem to make scrambled eggs when I'm lonely and sad. The contrast in textures between the slight chewiness of the mushrooms and the smoothness of the eggs has much the same effect as the French strive for in œufs brouillés, *for which they use truffles instead of mushrooms. The last time I bought truffles they were thirty dollars an ounce. The garlic is exactly what you need when cooking very simply for yourself. It makes you feel wanted.*

Using low heat is important with scrambled eggs to prevent them from sticking and becoming tough. To avoid overcooking scrambled eggs, never leave them on the burner until they look completely done, because they continue to cook with their own heat when they come out of the pan.

Serve these scrambled eggs on hot toast or with fresh asparagus or very lightly cooked slices of back bacon.

1 clove garlic
2 eggs
2 Tbsp [30 mL] cream or milk
½ tsp [2 mL] salt
3 Tbsp [45 mL] butter
¼ lb [125 g] fresh mushrooms, small or
    quartered
½ tsp [2 mL] tarragon
Freshly ground pepper

SLIGHTLY SQUASH THE GARLIC clove with the flat side of a knife and stick a fork into the garlic. In a bowl, lightly beat the eggs with the cream and salt, using the fork with the garlic clove attached. (Keeping the garlic clove on the fork forces you to beat the eggs lightly.) Set the egg mixture aside and discard garlic. Heat 2 Tbsp [30 mL] of the butter in a frying pan or heavy saucepan over medium heat, and cook the mushrooms with the tarragon and some pepper for 4 minutes, stirring gently. Add the remaining butter. As soon as it melts add the egg mixture. Reduce the heat to medium-low and cook slowly, stirring with mild determination until the eggs become stiff but are still moist. Serve immediately.

Scrambled eggs, with brown toast, are the world's best cure-all for the sniffles, the sads, the occasional broken heart and anything that ails you. —*Peasant's Alphabet*

EGGS AU NATUREL

EVERYBODY KNOWS HOW to boil an egg, but very few people know the secret of doing it well. Put the eggs (up to a dozen) in a saucepan, add cold water to cover them by 1 inch [2.5 cm], bring the water to a boil and turn off the heat. Let the eggs remain in the water for 15 minutes as it cools. They'll be perfectly cooked, easy to peel and less granular in texture than when cooked quickly, and they won't have that black line around the yolk. Put them back in the egg box and you have ready-to-go quick lunches. Hard-boiled eggs go very well tossed in a cabbage salad with lots of salt and chopped onion. Or cut them into chunks and mix them with slightly larger chunks of cold cooked potato, sprinkle with chopped parsley, olive oil, a dash of vinegar and a lot of pepper, and you have an instant potato salad that's a great improvement on the usual picnic offering.

I think the ultimate luxury is comfort. When I was a small boy, my allowance came from the chickens that preferred to lay their eggs in the garden, rather than the henhouse. We lived in the country, in a damp and chilly house, and almost every day in winter we sniffed and coughed and our noses ran. There was no heat in the house, except for a small fireplace in the kitchen, and for a lot of years (any time is a long time when you're eight years old) I crawled into bed in my clothes (my socks, pants, shirt and sweater). Slowly, as the bed warmed up, I took them off and kept them with me all night until one by one it was time to put them on again, get out of bed, and draw, with my finger, rude words in the frost on the inside of my window.

When it got too bad (my nose like a running tap and a face like a Christmas reindeer) my mother would decide that school was off for the day. Tomorrow I would take a note, but today I would spend in bed. "Nice and comfortable" she would say, and for that day only I would have a hot water bottle. In actual fact it was a brick, warmed in the oven and wrapped in two towels, and for perhaps half an hour it did help, giving a little comfort and a little warmth. Most of the day I lay stiff as a plank and cold as a fish, my chest rubbed with goose grease mixed with camphorated oil, and I thought seriously (and I remember, with some anticipation) of death. I hoped God would forget all the good things I'd done and remember only the bad, that he would be sure to send me to Hell, where at least it was warm.

But three times a day, on those long days in bed, real comfort arrived. My mother, no means the best cook, could boil an egg to perfection, not soft but not hard, and with it she would bring me toast cut into finger-wide strips. She cut the top off the egg and sat there, looking as happy as if she herself had laid it, while I dipped the toast into the egg and sucked it—rich and golden and warm and every mouthful telling me that life and love went on forever and that tomorrow, just because of the magic of the egg, I would be better. —*Peasant's Alphabet*

OMELETTE
`2 SERVINGS`

The quickest meal in any kitchen is an omelette—with practice you can turn out one a minute. The trick to a good omelette is keeping it light. And the secrets to that are first, don't put milk in it; second, have the pan hot enough; and third, use three eggs. A one-egg omelette gets tough, and one made with four eggs or more will burn on the bottom. Any fool can overcook an omelette.

3 eggs
Pinch of red pepper flakes
Pinch of salt
Water
1 Tbsp [15 mL] butter or vegetable oil

HEAT A FRYING PAN over medium heat. Crack the eggs into a bowl and add the red pepper flakes and salt. Fill half an eggshell with water and pour it into the egg mixture. Beat it very lightly with a fork, leaving some egg white and yolk visible. When the pan is hot, put in the butter and wave the pan about over the burner until the butter covers the bottom of the pan. Immediately pour in the eggs and stir them with the fork held flat and the tines pointing up, lifting the cooked eggs from the bottom to the top. When the eggs look shiny and still a bit liquid, fold over a third of the omelette in the pan, then flip the covered bit over the rest and tip the omelette onto a plate, where it will continue to cook.

Recollections of

BARBARA-JO MCINTOSH
COOKBOOK AUTHOR, OWNER OF BARBARA-JO'S BOOKS TO COOKS, VANCOUVER, BC

I really got to know James in 1990 when I opened my restaurant. He was a loyal supporter and came to dine many times, both with Chris and on his own. On Robbie Burns Day, he would delight customers by reading "Address to a Haggis." When James would write a favourable review, a lineup at the door was a certainty. I was grateful for all of this. And so it was inevitable that we would become close friends.

My favourite memory is from the summer of 2006. Chris was needed elsewhere and James was getting ready to go into the hospital for serious back surgery. None of us were sure he would make it through the ordeal. I travelled to his farm in Duncan to lend a hand. On the way there, I anticipated that he would order me around without mercy. This was his somewhat cranky way of acknowledging that I was a loved and trusted friend. No sooner had I arrived than I was ordered to feed the chickens and the donkeys before watering the vegetable garden. I was briefly permitted to freshen up before James commanded that I accompany him on a dizzying array of errands. I recall getting him into a large truck and then being ordered to drive. I had never driven a large truck before but—to James at least—this seemed a minor point.

It was a full day. The countryside was magical, the people we visited were charming and the village of Cowichan Bay seemed tailor-made for James to show off. That night, I cooked us a quiet dinner while James told me exactly how to prepare it. After the dishes were washed, I was allowed to go to bed. The next day, I returned to my position behind the wheel of the dreaded truck while James rode shotgun. Our mission? Drive to Victoria so that James could deliver his will to his lawyer. Of course, we had to stop for lunch. I was reluctant to have more than a sip of wine. But such prudence had no affect on my fellow drivers who continued to hurl abuse about my pathetic truck-driving abilities. Having clocked in another day of slavery, I was rewarded with a lovely dinner at a local winery.

Happily, James made it through the surgery. I was grateful for this, just as I was grateful for the opportunity to accommodate one of our country's most memorable culinary figures. Of course, being ordered around prompted a few curses under my breath. But the one thing James never had to do was order me to be his friend. That just happened naturally.

SWEET PEAR OMELETTE

2 SERVINGS

For breakfast, lunch or supper—an all-day reputation-maker.

2 Tbsp [30 mL] butter
2 pears, peeled, cored and sliced
1 Tbsp [15 mL] sugar
2 eggs, separated
1 Tbsp [15 mL] brandy

MELT THE BUTTER in a frying pan over medium heat. Add the pears and most of the sugar to the pan and cook for 2 to 3 minutes. Meanwhile, in a bowl beat the egg whites until they form stiff peaks. Fold the egg yolks into the egg whites and add the mixture to the pan. Cook for 2 to 3 minutes, until the egg is set. Turn the omelette out onto a plate, sprinkle it with the remaining sugar and drizzle the brandy over top.

TORTILLA ESPAÑOL (SPANISH POTATO OMELETTE)

4 SERVINGS

2 Tbsp [30 mL] olive oil
2 potatoes, cubed
1 onion, chopped
2 cloves garlic, chopped
4 eggs
1 tsp [5 mL] thyme
1 tsp [5 mL] pepper
½ tsp [2 mL] cayenne pepper
½ tsp [2 mL] salt
Chopped parsley

HEAT THE OIL in a frying pan and cook the potatoes until slightly softened. Add the onion and cook, stirring, until it is transparent. Add the garlic. In a bowl, beat the eggs with the thyme, pepper, cayenne and salt. Pour the egg mixture over the potatoes and cook until the eggs are set. Turn the omelette over and brown the other side. Serve sprinkled with parsley.

BANANA OMELETTE WITH APRICOT JAM

4 SERVINGS

2 bananas
Sugar
1 Tbsp [15 mL] butter
5 eggs, separated
Apricot jam

SLICE THE BANANAS and toss them in a bowl with some sugar. Melt the butter in a frying pan over medium heat and caramelize the bananas. Beat the egg yolks in one bowl. In another, whisk the egg whites until firm. Fold the yolks into the whites. Push the banana slices together into the centre of the pan and pour the egg mixture around them. Meanwhile, warm some apricot jam in a small saucepan. When the top of the omelette has set, serve it with the apricot jam as a sauce.

CURRIED ASPARAGUS EGGS WITH DILL

2 SERVINGS

1 Tbsp [15 mL] butter
½ tsp [2 mL] curry powder
1 bunch asparagus, stringy ends removed
Juice of ½ lemon
4 eggs
2 Tbsp [30 mL] chopped green onion
½ tsp [2 mL] dill
Salt and black pepper

MELT THE BUTTER in a frying pan over medium heat and stir in the curry powder. Cut the asparagus diagonally and add the pieces to the pan. Squeeze in the lemon juice and, when the asparagus is three-quarters cooked, remove the asparagus to a warm plate. In a bowl, lightly beat the eggs with the green onion, dill and some salt and black pepper. Pour the egg mixture into the frying pan and cook, stirring gently. When the eggs start to set, toss in the asparagus, stir and serve immediately.

BAKED EGGS, BULGARIAN STYLE

`2 SERVINGS`

1 Tbsp [15 mL] olive oil
1 tomato, sliced
4 oz [100 g] feta cheese
2 eggs
Pinch of paprika
Pinch of pepper
Pinch of salt
Sprig of oregano, chopped

PREHEAT OVEN TO 350F (180C). Pour the olive oil into a cold ovenproof frying pan or baking dish. Place the slices of tomato in the frying pan, and crumble half of the feta cheese over top. Break the eggs over the tomato and feta, and sprinkle with the remaining feta and some paprika, pepper and salt. Bake, uncovered, until the eggs are set and the feta has melted, about 10 minutes. Just before serving, sprinkle with oregano.

HUEVOS RANCHEROS

`2 SERVINGS`

Most recipes for Huevos Rancheros give you fussy directions to peel and seed tomatoes. That's all right if you've nothing else to do and you're not hungry. You want shortcuts. There's nothing wrong with canned tomatoes—Italians use them often. Tomatoes picked for canning are at their ripest and juiciest, and a can of diced tomatoes contains less juice and twice as much flesh as you'll get from a pound of tomatoes mucked about à la Martha Stewart.

Most recipes will also tell you to lightly fry the onion, then lightly fry the garlic (taking care not to brown or burn them), both of which take time that you can use for another purpose—like watching the moon rise. Onions need precooking to develop their taste in sauces,

but Italian cooks have a procedure they call battuto *(explained below) that requires no fuss and is burn-proof. This is a Mexican recipe, but Italians are the masters of quick cooking, so why not use their trick?*

Serve this egg dish with tortillas or bread or, if you're really hungry, a can of white beans.

2 cloves garlic, chopped
1 medium onion, coarsely chopped
¼ cup [50 mL] water
2 Tbsp [30 mL] peanut or grapeseed oil
½ tsp [2 mL] red pepper flakes or 1 tsp [5 mL] hot paprika
1 tsp [5 mL] dried thyme or oregano
1 can [14 oz/398 mL] diced tomatoes
1 tsp [5 mL] dried mint
4 large eggs
Salt and pepper

PUT THE GARLIC and onion in a frying pan with the water and oil. Bring the mixture to a boil and simmer for 2 to 3 minutes, until the water is almost gone (that's the battuto). Add the pepper flakes and thyme and stir for 2 seconds. Add the tomatoes and mint and bring to a quick boil. Meanwhile, crack the eggs into a saucer. Cook the sauce for 5 minutes, slide the eggs on top of the sauce, sprinkle with salt and pepper, cover and cook over medium heat until the eggs are ready (traditionally the yolks should still be runny). Slide them out of the pan and eat immediately.

VARIATIONS: Add 1 tsp [5 mL] cumin seeds or a bit of orange zest to the battuto before cooking. You could also add 1 Tbsp [15 mL] tomato paste to the tomatoes.

MUSHROOMS DIJON

4 SERVINGS

Eggs Benedict is incredible if cooked for two and served in bed and you have nothing to do the rest of the day. But in restaurants, with tired ham, soggy muffins, canned orange juice and domestic champagne, this gentle statement of love becomes as exciting as a Harlequin romance. And in the undersized, overcrowded kitchens of apartment dwellers who have to invite a lot of people to brunch because a lot of people invited them to brunch, preparing Eggs Benedict leads to nothing but panic and despair. Mushrooms Dijon, served on toasted rye bread or under poached eggs, is easier, cheaper and far nicer than Eggs Benedict. And different.

6 Tbsp [90 mL] butter
3 Tbsp [45 mL] lemon juice
1 lb [500 g] fresh mushrooms, small or
    quartered
½ cup [125 mL] water
½ tsp [2 mL] salt
3 Tbsp [45 mL] all-purpose flour
2 cups [500 mL] chicken stock or milk
2 to 3 oz [60–90 mL] sherry
1 tsp [5 mL] tarragon
1 tsp [5 mL] Dijon mustard
1 tsp [5 mL] powdered mustard
½ tsp [2 mL] water
½ tsp [2 mL] salt
½ tsp [2 mL] pepper
4 Tbsp [60 mL] whipping cream

PLACE 2 TBSP [30 mL] of the butter in a saucepan with 1 Tbsp [15 mL] of the lemon juice and the mushrooms, water and salt. Bring the mixture to a boil, cover and simmer for 5 minutes. Remove from the heat and let stand, uncovered, while you make the sauce.

    Melt the remaining butter in a heavy pan over medium-low heat. Add the flour and cook for 2 minutes, stirring vigorously. Pour in the chicken stock and sherry, add the tarragon and continue cooking, stirring until the mixture is smooth. In a bowl, mix the Dijon and powdered mustards with the water. Stir the mustard mixture into the sauce. Add the salt and pepper, stir well again and cook, covered, over the lowest heat for 15 minutes. Meanwhile, drain the mushroom mixture. Add the mushroom mixture, cream and remaining lemon juice to the sauce and stir well, heating a little more without letting the sauce boil. Serve with an air of modest virtue.

ALMOST EGGS FLORENTINE WITH EASY BÉCHAMEL

2 SERVINGS

"I love you."
"Great. Keep stirring."
"Really ..."
"I know. Let's eat."

1 tsp [5 mL] vegetable oil
½ onion, chopped
1 pkg frozen chopped spinach, thawed and
    drained, or 1 bunch fresh
Pepper
4 eggs
2 Tbsp [30 mL] butter
2 Tbsp [30 mL] all-purpose flour
1 cup [250 mL] milk
½ cup [125 mL] cream
Pinch of nutmeg
Pinch of salt

HEAT THE OIL in a frying pan over medium heat. Add the onion and cook for 2 to 3 minutes. Add the spinach and some pepper. Break the eggs onto a plate and gently slide the eggs onto the spinach. Cover and allow the eggs to poach for 5 minutes, or until the eggs are just set. In the meantime, melt the butter in a saucepan over medium heat. Add the flour and stir into a paste. Slowly pour in the milk, whisking to make sure no lumps form. Continue whisking as you bring the mixture to a boil. After it boils, add the cream and some nutmeg and salt. Bring to a boil again, pour the sauce over the poached eggs and serve.

HOMEMADE BREAKFAST SAUSAGE
`2 SERVINGS`

Serve these "sausages" for breakfast with eggs.

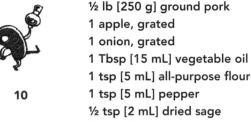

½ lb [250 g] ground pork
1 apple, grated
1 onion, grated
1 Tbsp [15 mL] vegetable oil
1 tsp [5 mL] all-purpose flour
1 tsp [5 mL] pepper
½ tsp [2 mL] dried sage
½ tsp [2 mL] salt
Vegetable oil

IN A BOWL, combine the pork, apple, onion, oil, flour, pepper, sage and salt. Form the mixture into small cakes. Fry them in oil over medium-high heat, until browned. Serve.

HOT DOUGHNUTS FOR BREAKFAST
`2 SERVINGS`

½ cup [125 mL] water
4 Tbsp [60 mL] butter
1 tsp [5 mL] sugar
¼ tsp [1 mL] salt
½ cup [125 mL] all-purpose flour
2 eggs
1 cup [250 mL] vegetable oil
Sugar

IN A SAUCEPAN, bring the water, butter, sugar and salt to a boil and immediately remove from the heat. Dump in the flour all at once and stir well. Add the eggs one at a time, mixing vigorously with a fork to make a very smooth batter. Cook the batter over the lowest heat, stirring until the batter no longer sticks to the sides of the saucepan. Heat the oil in a frying pan or saucepan over medium-high heat. Using two spoons, slide spoonfuls of the batter into the hot oil, leaving room for the doughnuts to puff up. Fry until medium brown, turning twice. Remove them from the oil with a fork, sprinkle with sugar and rush them (faster than a speeding bullet) to your best beloved with coffee or champagne, flowers, candles, love and kisses.

RICOTTA-STUFFED CANNELLONI WITH PEACHES
`4 SERVINGS`

8 cannelloni tubes
½ cup [125 g] ricotta cheese
1 can [14 oz/398 mL] peaches
2 Tbsp [30 mL] Cointreau, grappa or any
   orange liqueur

IN A LARGE POT of water, boil the cannelloni shells for 12 minutes. Drain. When the cannelloni are cool, slit them up the middle and stuff each with about 1 Tbsp [15 mL] ricotta cheese. Roll them up and arrange them on a plate. Place the peaches (with some of their juice) and Cointreau in a blender and blend until smooth. Pour this sauce over the stuffed cannelloni. Serve cold.

JAM BUTTIES
`1 SERVING`

In some parts of England, people eat chip butties—with french fries inside instead of jam. Serve the jam version with some yogurt.

Butter
2 slices bread
Jam
1 egg
2 Tbsp [30 mL] sugar

BUTTER BOTH SLICES of bread, spread one slice generously with jam and then put the slices together. Beat the egg in a bowl with 1 Tbsp [15 mL] sugar. Heat some butter in a frying pan over medium heat. Dip both sides of the butty in the egg (squish the butty a bit) and fry it in the butter until both sides are brown. Sprinkle with remaining sugar and serve.

Pancakes are a Saturday or Sunday indulgence, when you have time enough for one of you to stay in bed, while the other sits and reads the paper. There is nothing to the cooking of the pancakes; you just cook one side until there are bubbles on the top, turn it over and cook the other side and eat them with hot maple syrup and butter. They will keep warm wrapped in a cloth in a low oven until you get enough, or if you happen to have your bed in the kitchen you can just eat them as they come. There are people who spend Saturday night on an air mattress on the kitchen floor just to be there in the morning, but that is close to an addiction, which, until a local chapter of Pancakes Anonymous is formed, should be avoided.

But there are other aspects of these pancakes that should be noted. The first one up makes tea, peels an orange, gets the morning paper down off the roof and delivers these three things, preferably with flowers and a candle, to the bedside. He then puts on the coffee while he makes the pancake mixture, feeds the cat, avoids last night's dishes, and (this is a secret) sprinkles dry coffee on the stove burner so that the whole apartment begins to smell like coffee should taste.

By the time the coffee is ready the pancakes will be ready to cook. You know how to do this. Now, the first one you will have to try. Just to see if it is good enough for your mate. It will be. And perhaps that, you will think, was an accident, and you should try the next one.

So, you mix another batch, and finally deliver them, smiling, together with the maple syrup (if you can find Swedish lingonberries in a delicatessen then so much the better than anything else in the world), and butter, and hot coffee, and of course yourself, a portable radio and a couple of spare cushions.

The greatest pleasure comes in not answering the phone or the doorbell.
—*Ginger Tea Makes Friends*

OATMEAL BLUEBERRY PANCAKES

4 SERVINGS FOR KIDS OR 6 FOR ADULTS

How to be popular with kids.

2 cups [500 mL] buttermilk
½ cup [125 mL] quick-cooking oats
2 eggs
1 ½ cups [375 mL] all-purpose flour
1 Tbsp [15 mL] sugar
1 tsp [5 mL] baking soda
½ tsp [2 mL] cinnamon
Pinch of nutmeg
Pinch of salt
¾ cup [175 mL] blueberries
2 Tbsp [30 mL] vegetable oil
1 orange, sliced
Maple syrup

COMBINE THE BUTTERMILK and oats in a bowl and let stand for a few minutes. Then beat in the eggs. Add the flour, sugar, baking soda, cinnamon and some nutmeg and salt, and stir to combine. Stir in the blueberries. Heat the oil in a frying pan over medium heat and pour spoonfuls of the batter into the pan. Cook until bubbles form on the top of the pancakes, turn them and cook the other side until lightly browned. Serve with orange slices and maple syrup.

heat until water

bounces

OATMEAL FLAPJACKS WITH WHISKEY PRUNE SAUCE

How to be popular with adults.

VARIATION: If you want to make the sauce a savoury, spicy one, add ½ tsp [2 mL] cayenne pepper. To make it stickier for use on barbecued meat, chicken or fish, mix 1 Tbsp [15 mL] cornstarch with the whiskey and add for the last 2 minutes of cooking time.

SAUCE
1 cup [250 mL] pitted prunes, finely chopped
¾ cup [175 mL] water
2 Tbsp [30 mL] molasses, honey or brown sugar
2 Tbsp [30 mL] whiskey
½ tsp [2 mL] cinnamon
½ tsp [2 mL] powdered ginger

PLACE THE PRUNES, water, molasses, whiskey, cinnamon and ginger in a saucepan deep enough to allow the sauce to bubble up. Simmer for 5 minutes. Set aside.

FLAPJACKS
1 egg
¾ cup [175 mL] rolled oats (not instant)
½ cup [125 mL] all-purpose flour
1 tsp [5 mL] baking soda
½ tsp [2 mL] salt
Buttermilk
1 Tbsp [15 mL] vegetable oil

IN A BOWL, mix the egg, oats, flour, baking soda and salt with enough buttermilk to form a thick batter. Heat the oil in a frying pan over medium heat and drop in spoonfuls of the batter. Pat them down and cook until they rise slightly and are lightly browned. Serve with Whiskey Prune Sauce.

BRUSCHETTA WITH FRUIT

1 cup [250 mL] ricotta or cottage cheese
2 Tbsp [30 mL] orange juice
1 baguette, sliced into finger-thick pieces
12 grapes, halved
6 strawberries, sliced
2 peaches, sliced, or 1 can [14 oz/398 mL] peaches, drained
4 Tbsp [60 mL] brown sugar
Sprig of fresh mint

IN A BOWL, mix the ricotta and orange juice together. Toast the baguette and spread the cheese on the warm bread. Top with grape halves and slices of strawberry and peach, and sprinkle with brown sugar. Serve garnished with mint leaves.

PAIN PERDU

A New Orleans version of French toast. Serve it with butter and maple syrup.

3 Tbsp [45 mL] vegetable oil
3 eggs
3 Tbsp [45 mL] sugar
2 Tbsp [30 mL] rum or whiskey
1 Tbsp [15 mL] milk
Zest of ½ lemon
6 slices day-old bread
Icing sugar

HEAT THE OIL in a frying pan over medium heat. In a bowl, beat together the eggs, sugar, rum, milk and lemon zest. Dredge the bread slices in this mixture and place them carefully in the hot frying pan. Fry for 3 to 4 minutes on each side, or until golden brown. Sprinkle with icing sugar and serve.

I PREFER IT WITHOUT SCOTCH

OR RUM

STARTERS & SNACKS

Candied Walnut Halves, 15

Spiced Peanuts, 15

Baked Garlic, 15

Baked Olives, 15

Baked Parmesan Fennel, 15

Baked Feta, 16

Mayonnaise (Three Colours), 16

Real Guacamole, 16

Eggplant Dip, 16

The Ultimate Chips and Dip, 17

Pepper Pitas, 17

Hummus on the Cheap, 17

White Bean Ful, 17

Falafel, 18

Poor Man's Escargots, 18

Oysters with Whiskey, 18

Clams Daniel, 19

Mussels with Beer, 19

Cinda Chavich's Mussels with Lime, Gin and Juniper, 21

Slightly Spicy Scallops, 22

Prawns in Beer, 22

Fish Cakes, 22

La Bodega Callos a la Madrileña (Madrid-Style Tripe), 23

Calamari in Beer Batter, 24

Tzatziki, 24

Ground Lamb Balls with Cherries, 24

Spicy Chicken Wings, 25

Satay, 25

Tofu and Red Onions in Pita, 26

CANDIED WALNUT HALVES

1 cup [250 mL] walnut halves
4 Tbsp [60 mL] sugar
Pinch of cayenne pepper
2 Tbsp [30 mL] vegetable oil

BLANCH THE WALNUTS in boiling water, drain and toss with the sugar and cayenne pepper. Heat the oil in a frying pan and fry the walnuts for 4 to 5 minutes over high heat until they are glistening. Take care not to darken them, which will make them bitter. Allow to cool. Store in an airtight jar.

SPICED PEANUTS

MAKES 1 CUP [250 ML]

1 cup [250 mL] dry-roasted unsalted peanuts
2 tsp [10 mL] olive oil
½ tsp [2 mL] curry powder
½ tsp [2 mL] salt

HEAT THE PEANUTS in a dry frying pan over medium heat. Add oil and curry powder, stir well and cook for 2 minutes. Tip out onto a paper towel and sprinkle with salt.

BAKED GARLIC

2 SERVINGS

1 head garlic, unpeeled
Olive oil
Red wine

PREHEAT OVEN TO 300F [150C]. Place the whole head of garlic in the middle of a doubled piece of foil and form the foil into a package, leaving the top open. Drizzle some olive oil and wine over the garlic. Bake for 30 to 45 minutes. Peel the cloves and mash them onto some bread or serve as a side dish.

BAKED OLIVES

MAKES 1 CUP [250 ML]

1 clove garlic, chopped
1 cup [250 mL] black oil-cured olives (not canned)
¼ cup [50 mL] white wine
1 Tbsp [15 mL] olive oil

IN A FRYING PAN, combine the garlic, olives, wine and oil. Cook, covered, for 5 minutes over medium heat. Put the olives in a dish and be surprised at how pleased your guests are to eat them.

BAKED PARMESAN FENNEL

4 SERVINGS

An appetizer straight from Milan—just don't use packaged supermarket Parmesan or you'll think it came straight from Sarnia.

2 Tbsp [30 mL] dried bread crumbs
2 Tbsp [30 mL] grated Parmesan cheese
1 clove garlic, chopped
½ tsp [2 mL] rosemary
Salt and pepper
1 egg
2 fennel bulbs, trimmed and sliced lengthwise
3 Tbsp [45 mL] olive oil

PREHEAT OVEN TO 400F [200C]. In a shallow bowl, mix together the bread crumbs, Parmesan, garlic and rosemary, and season with salt and pepper. In another bowl, beat the egg. Dip the fennel slices first in the beaten egg and then in the bread crumb mixture. Lay the fennel slices in a greased baking dish, drizzle with olive oil and bake for 15 to 20 minutes.

BAKED FETA
2 SERVINGS

¼ lb [125 g] feta or goat cheese
1 Tbsp [15 mL] olive oil
½ tsp [2 mL] red pepper flakes
Pepper

PREHEAT OVEN TO 400F [200C]. Cut the cheese into ½-inch (1 cm) thick slices and place them in an ungreased baking dish. Drizzle with half of the olive oil and sprinkle with the red pepper flakes and some pepper. Bake, uncovered, until just melted, about 8 to 10 minutes. Serve with the remaining olive oil drizzled over top.

MAYONNAISE (THREE COLOURS)

HAVE READY some cherry tomatoes, hard-boiled eggs and chopped parsley. Make three types of mayonnaise by placing 2 Tbsp [30 mL] mayonnaise in each of three small bowls. Mix 1 tsp [5 mL] curry powder into one bowl, mix 1 tsp [5 mL] tomato paste into the second bowl and to the third add 1 tsp [5 mL] each of curry powder and tomato paste, stirring to blend. Arrange the three different colours of mayonnaise on a platter and scatter with cherry tomatoes. Halve the hard-boiled eggs and arrange on the mayonnaise. Garnish with chopped parsley.

REAL GUACAMOLE
MAKES ABOUT 1 CUP [250 ML]

You know what guacamole is—and it's usually more complicated than this. You know better.

2 avocados, peeled, pitted and mashed
1 small onion, finely chopped
Juice of 1 lime
Salt and pepper

IN A BOWL, mash the avocado with a fork and combine with the onion, lime juice and some salt and pepper. Serve.

EGGPLANT DIP
MAKES ABOUT 2 CUPS [500 ML]

1 medium eggplant, whole
1 clove garlic
½ cup [125 mL] yogurt
2 Tbsp [30 mL] chopped cilantro or parsley
1 Tbsp [15 mL] sesame seeds
½ tsp [2 mL] cumin
Juice of 1 lemon
Salt and pepper

PREHEAT OVEN TO 400F [200C]. Bake the eggplant for 30 minutes, or until soft. Cut the eggplant in half and scoop the flesh out into a food processor. Add the garlic, yogurt, cilantro, sesame seeds, cumin and lemon juice, and process until smooth. Season with salt and pepper and serve with Pepper Pitas (page 17).

Eggplants are surely the most beautiful of all the vegetables. Plump, shiny and as overblown as costume jewellery, some are round, some are egg-shaped, some are long and skinny, but no matter how they come they are so complete and so perfect that the most healthy of them might be easily artificial.
The eggplant's greatest virtue is its ability to absorb. Oils, spices, butter, flavours and the other energies of the kitchen: the eggplant not only takes them, but amplifies and extends them. Eggplants give you feedback—the more you put in, the more you get back. A really good melitzano (the eggplant popular in Greek restaurants) contains as many as eighteen herbs and spices, all of them slightly improved by association with the bland and sleeping beauty of their host.
—*Peasant's Alphabet*

THE ULTIMATE CHIPS AND DIP
MAKES ABOUT 1 CUP [250 ML]

½ lb [250 g] feta or goat cheese
¼ cup [50 mL] olive oil
Zest and juice of ½ lemon
½ tsp [2 mL] red pepper flakes
Pepper
Black olives
Pita bread

PLACE THE CHEESE, 3 Tbsp [45 mL] of the olive oil and the lemon zest and juice in a food processor. Purée until smooth. Transfer the mixture to a serving bowl. Stir in the red pepper flakes and season with pepper. Drizzle the remaining olive oil over top just before serving. Serve with olives and wedges of pita bread. For a thicker dip, refrigerate the cheese mixture for several hours or overnight. It can be stored, refrigerated, for about a week.

PEPPER PITAS
MAKES 32 PITA WEDGES

8 pita breads
4 Tbsp [60 mL] olive oil
2 Tbsp [30 mL] chopped parsley
2 Tbsp [30 mL] pepper
Pinch of salt

PREHEAT OVEN TO 400F [200C]. Cut the pita into quarters. Brush with oil and sprinkle with parsley, pepper and a little salt. Bake until crisp, about 5 minutes.

HUMMUS ON THE CHEAP
MAKES ABOUT 2 CUPS [500 ML]

Tahini is expensive, so I use peanut butter. It smooths this hummus out a bit and gives it a rich flavour.

1 can [14 oz/398 mL] chickpeas, rinsed and drained
3 cloves garlic
6 Tbsp [90 mL] yogurt
4 Tbsp [60 mL] peanut butter
Juice of 1 lemon

IN A FOOD PROCESSOR, combine the chickpeas, garlic, yogurt, peanut butter and lemon juice, processing until smooth. For a thinner hummus, dilute the mixture with a little warm water, more lemon juice or more yogurt.

WHITE BEAN FUL
4 SERVINGS

In Egypt, this bean purée is a popular breakfast dish, but sometimes it is served as an appetizer. Serve it with pita bread, hard-boiled eggs and lemon wedges.

1 can [14 oz/398 mL] white beans, rinsed and drained
5 cloves garlic, chopped
2 tomatoes, chopped
1 cup [250 mL] parsley, chopped
⅓ cup [75 mL] vegetable oil
Zest and juice of 2 lemons
Salt and pepper

IN A FOOD PROCESSOR combine all ingredients and process until smooth.

LEMON

17

Starters & Snacks

FALAFEL

4 SERVINGS

A Lebanese treat. Serve it with pita bread, hummus and chopped tomatoes and cucumbers.

1 can [28 oz/796 mL] chickpeas, drained
1 egg
2 cloves garlic
2 green onions, chopped
½ onion, chopped
⅓ cup [75 mL] chopped mint
3 Tbsp [45 mL] all-purpose flour
1 tsp [5 mL] baking powder
1 tsp [5 mL] coriander
1 tsp [5 mL] cumin
½ tsp [2 mL] turmeric
¼ tsp [1 mL] cayenne pepper
Salt and pepper
Vegetable oil

IN A FOOD PROCESSOR, combine the chickpeas, egg, garlic, green onion, onion, mint, flour, baking powder, coriander, cumin, turmeric, cayenne pepper and some salt and pepper, making sure the mixture stays grainy and does not become mushy. Transfer the mixture to a bowl and let stand for 1 hour. Roll the mixture into small balls. Heat ¾ inch [2 cm] oil in a deep frying pan and drop the falafel balls into it, cooking them until brown and crispy on all sides. Serve.

POOR MAN'S ESCARGOTS

4 SERVINGS

Snails served in restaurants, even if the menu does call them escargots, tend to a certain rubberiness that you have to endure for the sake of later sopping up the snail butter. I make snail butter in large quantities, freeze it and cook small trout or fillets of chicken breast in it. Sometimes I put it on steamed carrots or broad beans. Most of all, I like it with mushrooms because a fresh, not overcooked mushroom almost recreates the tender chewiness of the fresh snails served by the bowlful in Marseilles. Be generous with the butter and serve with good bread for sopping it up.

4 cloves garlic, finely chopped
3 Tbsp [45 mL] finely chopped parsley
2 Tbsp [30 mL] finely chopped chives
½ cup [125 mL] butter
1 Tbsp [15 mL] olive oil
½ tsp [2 mL] pepper
Juice of ¼ lemon
½ lb [250 g] medium mushrooms

PREHEAT OVEN TO 450F [230C]. In a bowl, mash the garlic, parsley and chives into the butter with a fork. Add the olive oil, pepper and lemon juice, and mash the butter some more. This is snail butter. (If you double the quantity, you can make the butter in a blender or food processor.) Remove the mushroom stalks and fill the caps with snail butter. Bake for 6 to 8 minutes. The mushroom caps can also be broiled for 6 minutes instead of baked. Alternatively, smear the bottom of an electric frying pan with a little oil and cook the stuffed mushrooms, covered, for 6 minutes.

OYSTERS WITH WHISKEY

MAKES 6 TO 8 OYSTERS

Sinful and delicious.

1 Tbsp [15 mL] butter
⅔ cup [150 mL] bread crumbs
Salt and pepper
2 Tbsp [30 mL] olive oil
Juice of ½ lemon
1 Tbsp [15 mL] whiskey
6 to 8 raw oysters, shucked
Cracked ice
Lemon wedges

MELT THE BUTTER in a frying pan over medium heat and gently brown the bread crumbs. Season with salt and pepper.

In a small bowl, mix together the olive oil, lemon juice and whiskey and drizzle over the oysters. Spoon the fried bread crumbs on top of each oyster. Serve on cracked ice with lemon wedges.

CLAMS DANIEL

MAKES ABOUT 1 CUP [250 ML]

Scoop up this wonderful concoction with tortilla chips.

1 Tbsp [15 mL] olive oil
1 clove garlic, finely chopped
1 medium onion, finely chopped
1 tsp [5 mL] pepper
½ tsp [2 mL] curry powder
1 can [7 oz/200 mL] baby clams
1 Tbsp [15 mL] sherry
Juice of ½ lemon
Chopped parsley

HEAT THE OIL in a frying pan over medium heat, and fry the garlic and onion until transparent. Add pepper and curry powder, and stir well. Drain the clams (reserve the clam juice and drink it mixed with vodka). Toss the clams into the pan and pour in the sherry and lemon juice. Cook for 2 minutes. Serve sprinkled with parsley.

MUSSELS WITH BEER

4 SERVINGS

2 lb [1 kg] cultured mussels
1 Tbsp [15 mL] vegetable oil
1 sweet red pepper, sliced
1 small onion, sliced
2 cloves garlic, minced
A few sprigs of thyme, chopped
1 cup [250 mL] lager beer
¼ tsp [1 mL] salt

RINSE THE MUSSELS under cold running water to remove any grit, and pull out any beards (the stringy bits attached to some of the mussels). Discard any mussels that are not tightly closed. Heat the oil in a large pot over medium-high heat. Cook the pepper and onion until they are soft. Stir in the garlic and thyme, and cook for 1 minute. Toss in the mussels, pour the beer over top and stir in the salt. (Drink the beer left in the bottle.) Cover, bring the mixture to a boil, reduce the heat to a simmer and let the mussels steam for about 5 minutes. Discard any mussels that have not opened. Take care not overcook the mussels, which will make them tough and leathery. Serve.

Daniel was a waiter. And Daniel liked to eat. He liked to eat a little more and a little better than most people. So he learned to cook. Which made him an even better waiter because when people asked him "What is...?" he would tell them. They would be impressed because he had a French accent, surprised to get an answer, and generally grateful because waiters sometimes tend to put their noses on high beam and make you feel stupid. Their gratitude made Daniel a lot of money. He decided to become a restaurateur, to open his own joint, to become the employer of waiters. And then make much more money, in much less time. But Daniel found that it would have been easier to walk across Lake Ontario than to make money in a restaurant, and that operating a twenty-four-hour daycare centre would have given him more time. Daniel now runs a fishing boat. He makes this dish for himself. He used to make it for his customers. Nobody knew it came out of a can. And if you don't tell them either... —*Fear of Frying*

CINDA CHAVICH

FOOD JOURNALIST AND AUTHOR

By the time I actually met James Barber, like many people I felt like I already knew him.

That's probably because I had spent so many afternoons with James, watching him (and Martin Yan and Graham Kerr) whip up simple recipes and impart culinary wisdom on the box. I grew up on the Canadian prairies, eons before celebrity chefs and food porn networks, but James—a true culinary raconteur—was beamed into my life during those formative years and obviously I was listening.

Like James, I never trained as a chef, but it might have been scribbling down his recipes in the rumpus room after school that started me on this course of scribbling down recipes and notes and techniques, and poking my nose into kitchens and pots around the world.

I was lucky enough to bump into James during my own food-writing career, even to travel with him once on a rollicking road trip to investigate the origins of gin in southern England. My memories are a happy blur of blending gin in beakers in Plymouth; elegant martinis at The Dukes, mad mixologists at Dick's Bar and sipping pink gin cocktails, bathed in funky fuchsia lighting, at Jamie Oliver's Fifteen. James's knowing and sometimes caustic commentary on the country of his birth, which inspired this seductive spirit we both loved, added much to the ride.

I'm not sure there was a single James Barber recipe that inspired me, but rather it was his unpretentious approach to the subject of food that invited me to join the party. I was always bowled over by his presence, his writing, his freely shared knowledge and his candour. With his no-nonsense, forge-ahead style, James really did take the fear out of frying.

He loved food—and life and donkeys and cats—and had a wonderful wicked side, as well as a very sensible, centred one. He tried to teach me about deep yoga breathing on a train (after observing my stress level) and candidly regaled me with stories about the best (and worst) restaurants and food producers in his corner of Vancouver Island when I chanced upon him having coffee in Cowichan Bay last summer, 2007. That was the last time I was lucky enough to share an hour with James. We talked about cheese and wine and good chefs (and pretentious nits) and how a good bakery, like the one in this tiny town, centres a community. I didn't have time to visit him at his farm that day, but he told me about his olive trees and the first wild greens of spring and the sadness of losing his favourite donkey.

James didn't suffer fools, but he was generous and wise and lived his life with the same irreverence and pure passion that came through in his distinctive delivery on television. He taught us all that cooking—and eating—is one of life's pleasures, to be shared and enjoyed to the fullest every day. A good gin martini doesn't hurt either.

Lesson learned.

CINDA CHAVICH'S MUSSELS WITH LIME, GIN AND JUNIPER

8 APPETIZER OR 4 MAIN-COURSE SERVINGS

I collected this recipe on our gin trip to the historic distillery in Plymouth. In true Barber style, it's rich, zesty and super-simple. Use one of the premium gins, such as Plymouth or Hendrick's. Serve the mussels with lots of crusty bread to mop up the juices.

4 lb (2 kg) fresh mussels
4 Tbsp [60 mL] butter
4 juniper berries, crushed
4 shallots, minced
¼ cup [50 mL] gin
Zest, finely grated, and juice of 3 small limes
1 cup [250 mL] crème fraîche,
    or ½ cup [125 mL] whipping cream
    and ½ cup [125 mL] sour cream
Salt and freshly ground black pepper
½ cup [125 mL] chopped chervil
½ cup [125 mL] chopped Italian parsley
1 tsp [5 mL] Asian chili paste (optional)

SCRUB THE MUSSELS in cold water, pull off the beards and scrape off any barnacles from the shells. Discard any mussels that are broken or don't close tightly when tapped on the counter.

Melt the butter in a large frying pan or wok. Add the crushed juniper berries and shallots, and cook for 5 minutes over medium-low heat until softened. Pour in the gin and bring the mixture to a boil. Add the lime zest and juice and the mussels; cover and cook over high heat for 3 to 4 minutes, just until the mussels open. Discard any that do not open.

Tip the mussels into a large colander set over a bowl to catch the cooking juices. Strain the juices through a fine sieve and put the mussels in a warm serving dish.

Pour the strained juices into a clean pan, whisk in the crème fraîche and heat through. Season with salt and pepper, and stir in half the chervil and parsley. Add the chili paste if you like a bit of zing in your food. Pour the sauce over the mussels in the dish and sprinkle with the remaining chervil and parsley. Share.

SLIGHTLY SPICY SCALLOPS
2 SERVINGS

1 egg yolk
½ cup [125 mL] whipping cream
1 tsp [5 mL] salt
½ tsp [2 mL] pepper
¼ cup [50 mL] butter
8 sea scallops or 16 bay scallops
½ tsp [2 mL] curry powder
½ cup [125 mL] white wine

IN A BOWL, combine the egg yolk and ¼ cup [50 mL] of the cream with the salt and pepper. Set aside. Melt the butter in a frying pan over medium heat. Place the scallops in the frying pan and cook them for about 2 minutes. Remove the scallops from the pan and set them aside. Sprinkle the curry powder in the same frying pan and add the wine. Bring to a boil, and stir in the remaining cream. Reduce the heat to low. Pour the egg mixture slowly into the pan while stirring quickly, so the egg doesn't curdle. Return the scallops to the pan, cook for 2 minutes and serve.

PRAWNS IN BEER
4 SERVINGS

2 lb [1 kg] fresh, uncooked prawns with their
    shells on
1 bottle of beer
1 Tbsp [15 mL] dill
1 Tbsp [15 mL] vegetable oil
1 or 2 fresh fennel bulbs, sliced
1 lemon, cut into wedges
Freshly ground black pepper

ABOUT 1 HOUR before cooking the prawns, put them in a bowl with the beer and dill and allow to marinate. Afterwards, heat the oil in a frying pan and sauté the fennel slices until browned on each side. When the fennel is almost cooked, heat another frying pan without oil until the pan is very hot. Remove the prawns from the marinade and place them in the dry pan. Sear until their skins change colour, about 1 minute on each side. Serve the fennel slices with the prawns, garnished with lemon wedges and pepper.

FISH CAKES
4 APPETIZER OR 2 MAIN-COURSE SERVINGS

Canned salmon, canned tuna or leftover fish or crab— all make good fish cakes. Purists make their fish cakes with fish and potatoes; others substitute cooked rice for the potatoes. There are three secrets to making fish cakes: first, use the right proportions of potato (or rice) and fish; second, eat them as they come out of the pan; third (very important), make sure the cook gets a proper share. Serve them with ketchup, Worcestershire sauce, salsa or a slice of crisp fried bacon.

2 cups [500 mL] cold mashed potatoes
1 cup [250 mL] canned salmon, tuna
    or cold cooked fish
1 egg
1 medium onion, finely chopped
½ tsp [2 mL] pepper
Handful of chopped parsley
Bread crumbs or all-purpose flour
2 Tbsp [30 mL] oil for frying

IN A BOWL, combine the potato, fish, egg, onion, pepper and parsley. Roll the mixture into balls as large as eggs. Flatten each ball into a round as thick as your finger and dredge in bread crumbs. In a frying pan over medium heat, fry the cakes in oil for a few minutes, until crisp and brown. Serve.

The Genius of James Barber

JOSÉ AND PACO RIVAS

OWNERS, LA BODEGA, VANCOUVER, BC

This is the same tapa recipe that we use at La Bodega, where James would often come to eat this delicious dish—he liked all kinds of entrails.

LA BODEGA CALLOS A LA MADRILEÑA
(MADRID-STYLE TRIPE)

4 SERVINGS

2 pig's feet
2 lb [1 kg] honeycomb tripe (parboiled variety
   commonly available in supermarkets)
2 Tbsp [30 mL] olive oil
1 medium onion, finely chopped
2 cloves garlic, finely chopped
1 cup [250 mL] chopped dry chorizo sausage
¼ cup [50 mL] white wine
Dash of paprika
Salt and pepper
Chopped parsley

BOIL THE PIG'S FEET and tripe in a large pot of water, covered, for about 2 ½ hours, or until tender. Drain, retaining the stock. Once cool, cut the tripe into small squares and debone the feet, cutting the meat into small pieces. Set aside.

Heat the olive oil in a pot over medium heat and cook the onion until it is transparent. Add the garlic and chorizo and and cook for about 2 minutes. Add the wine, paprika, pig's feet, tripe and just enough of the reserved stock to cover, and bring the mixture to a boil. Season with salt and pepper, and garnish with parsley. Serve.

CALAMARI IN BEER BATTER

Serve these crisp calamari rings with lemon wedges, chopped parsley and tzatziki (this page). If you don't want to make the batter, simply dip the squid rings into seasoned flour before frying.

1 lb [500 g] cleaned calamari (squid)
1 egg
1 cup [250 mL] all-purpose flour
½ cup [125 mL] beer
1 tsp [5 mL] oregano
½ tsp [2 mL] salt
Freshly ground pepper
Vegetable oil

CUT THE BODIES of the squid into ½-inch [1 cm] rings. In a bowl, combine the egg, flour, beer, oregano, salt and some pepper. Pour enough oil into a high-sided pan to fill it one-third full. Heat the oil until hot. Dip the squid rings into the batter and then into the hot oil, cooking them for only 1 or 2 minutes. Take care not to overcook them or put too many in the pan at once. Drain the squid on paper towels before serving.

TZATZIKI
MAKES ABOUT 2 CUPS [500 ML]

1 grated cucumber or zucchini
1 cup [250 mL] plain yogurt
½ tsp [2 mL] dried oregano or dill
  or 1 tsp [5 mL] chopped fresh
½ tsp [2 mL] pepper
½ tsp [2 mL] salt

IN A BOWL, combine the cucumber with the yogurt, oregano, pepper and salt.

GROUND LAMB BALLS WITH CHERRIES
MAKES ABOUT 24 MEATBALLS

These meatballs go well with pita bread.

1 lb [500 g] ground lamb
½ tsp [2 mL] cinnamon
½ tsp [2 mL] cloves
½ tsp [2 mL] nutmeg
Salt and pepper
2 Tbsp [30 mL] olive oil
½ lb [250 g] pitted cherries, fresh or canned
1 tsp [5 mL] orange zest
Juice of lemon
½ tsp [2 mL] sugar (if using fresh cherries)

IN A BOWL, use your hands to mix the meat with the cinnamon, cloves, nutmeg and some salt and pepper until the mixture is smooth. Form it into small balls. Heat the oil in a frying pan and fry the meatballs until golden brown. Meanwhile, in a saucepan heat the cherries with the orange zest, lemon juice and sugar (if using fresh cherries). Add the sautéed meatballs and simmer gently until cooked through. Add more liquid if necessary. Serve.

Lamb is a good thing to start being adventurous with—in a stew or on a barbecue or even in a lamburger. It marries well with almost anything: tomatoes, most herbs, apples, potatoes, garlic, red wine, peppers and beans.

I once ate a wonderful stew of lamb and peanuts in Northern China, and since then I've taken to spreading peanut butter on barbecued lamb chops. —*Cooking for Two*

This recipe is certainly not for WASP cocktail parties or indeed any party where white gloves are required. This chicken is sticky, messy and wonderful, and I like to go at it sitting around a table with a couple of good friends and a little Jack Daniels Black. But if you want to make these wings for a party, get everything ready beforehand and be prepared to stand at the stove making batches as fast as people eat them.

That's how you establish a reputation.
—*Flash in the Pan*

SPICY CHICKEN WINGS

MAKES 20

20 chicken wings
3 to 4 cloves garlic, finely chopped
2 Tbsp [30 mL] brown sugar
1 Tbsp [15 mL] dry mustard
½ bottle beer
1 Tbsp [15 mL] sesame oil
1 Tbsp [15 mL] soy sauce
1 tsp [5 mL] vinegar
Chopped parsley
Sesame seeds

CUT THE CHICKEN wings across at the joints, discarding the tips or keeping them to use for stock. Heat a dry frying pan over high heat. Place the chicken wings in the pan and brown them lightly on each side. Reduce the heat to medium and stir in the garlic, brown sugar, mustard and beer. Cook for 5 to 8 minutes, making sure that the chicken wings are well coated with the sauce. Add the sesame oil, soy sauce and vinegar, stir well and cook for a further 5 minutes. Add more beer if the sauce gets too thick. Serve on a platter sprinkled with parsley and sesame seeds.

SATAY

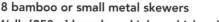

MAKES 8 SKEWERS

You can cook satay on the barbecue or in the oven—I've even used a toaster oven. Pork or beef can also be used for satay.

8 bamboo or small metal skewers
½ lb [250 g] boneless skinless chicken breast, cut into bite-sized pieces
Juice of ½ lemon
1 chili, finely chopped or ½ tsp [2 mL] dried chili flakes
1 clove garlic, finely chopped
3 Tbsp [45 mL] water
1 Tbsp [15 mL] vegetable oil
1 Tbsp [15 mL] peanut butter
1 tsp [5 mL] soy sauce
1 tsp [5 mL] tomato paste

SOAK THE BAMBOO skewers in water for 30 minutes. Preheat the broiler. Place 3 or 4 pieces of meat on each skewer and sprinkle with lemon juice. Combine the chili, garlic, water, oil, peanut butter, soy sauce and tomato paste in a small saucepan. Cook the mixture over medium heat for 2 to 3 minutes, stirring until smooth. Set aside. Cook the meat under the broiler for 3 minutes on each side, or until the meat is done. Serve the satay as an appetizer with the sauce, hot or cold.

TOFU AND RED ONIONS IN PITA
2 SERVINGS

Even though you can't find tofu in Greece, this chunky filling is very Greek.

1 Tbsp [15 mL] olive oil
1 clove garlic, finely chopped
1 red onion, thinly sliced
½ pkg [500 g pkg] medium tofu, sliced
1 Tbsp [15 mL] soy sauce
Juice of half a lemon
Pinch of cayenne
2 pita breads, cut in half
Lettuce or spinach leaves, washed and dried
2 Tbsp [30 mL] yogurt
1 avocado, peeled and sliced

HEAT THE OIL in a frying pan over high heat. Add the garlic, onion and tofu and cook until lightly browned. Stir in the soy sauce, lemon juice and cayenne. Open up the pita breads and line the insides with lettuce leaves. Pile the tofu mixture into the pitas and top with yogurt and slices of avocado.

SALADS

Cabbage 101, 29

Avocado Ginaigrette, 29

Fennel Salad, 29

Venetian Orange and Onion Salad, 29

Curried Cantaloupe, 29

Fresh Asparagus with Strawberry Vinaigrette, 30

Greens with Warm Pear and Walnut Dressing, 30

Dandelion and Spinach Salad, 30

Hot Salad of Sweet Peppers, 31

Chickpea Vinaigrette, 31

Lentil Salad, 31

Peruvian Potato Salad, 32

Thai Papaya Salad, 32

Fried Prawns and Mango Salad, 32

Spinach Salad with Feta and Oranges, 32

Hot Bacon Salad, 33

Zucchini and Mint Salad, 33

CABBAGE 101

A HEAD OF LETTUCE will go limp overnight, but a good, big green cabbage will keep, unrefrigerated, for the better part of a week uncut, and three or four days cut, if wrapped tightly in a plastic bag. Cut the cabbage into big wedges, then grate them on the coarse side of the grater, grate some carrot to go with the cabbage and toss it with a quick dressing of peanut butter, salt, pepper, a pinch of sugar and whatever you have available to drink (apple juice, beer, sherry, white wine, orange juice—they all work with cabbage). You can dress it up with thinly sliced apple or a few of your cocktail-hour peanuts (or walnuts, almonds or whatever you've got) or toss in a can of sockeye or tuna for a quick summer lunch. Shredded cabbage is foolproof and indestructible.

AVOCADO GINAIGRETTE
4 SERVINGS

2 avocados
3 Tbsp [45 mL] olive oil
1 Tbsp [15 mL] gin
Juice of ½ lemon
½ tsp [2 mL] cayenne pepper
Salt and pepper
1 egg yolk

PEEL AND SLICE the avocados and arrange on a plate. Pour the oil, gin and lemon juice into a jar and add the cayenne and some salt and pepper. Put the lid on the jar and shake well. Add the egg yolk and shake well again to form mayonnaise. Pour over the avocados and serve.

FENNEL SALAD
4 SERVINGS

1 fennel bulb
1 Tbsp [15 mL] olive oil
Juice of ½ orange
Salt and pepper

CUT THE FENNEL bulb lengthwise into quarters, and then slice them crosswise as thin as you can. In a bowl, toss the fennel with the olive oil, orange juice and some salt and pepper. Let stand for 10 minutes. Serve after your main course.

VENETIAN ORANGE AND ONION SALAD
2 SERVINGS

Use nice, juicy oranges in this salad.

3 oranges, peeled and thinly sliced
1 red onion, thinly sliced
Olive oil
Salt and pepper

TOSS THE ORANGES and onion together in a bowl. Drizzle the oil over top, sprinkle with a bit of salt and pepper and serve.

CURRIED CANTALOUPE
4 SERVINGS

1 cantaloupe
1 cucumber, cubed
2 Tbsp [30 mL] oil
1 tsp curry powder
½ tsp [2 mL] salt
Juice of 1 lemon

CUT THE MELON in half, scoop out the flesh and cut it into cubes. Put the melon and cucumber cubes in a bowl. In a frying pan over medium heat, stir together the oil, curry powder, salt and lemon juice. When the mixture is hot and well-combined, pour it over the melon and cucumber, and toss. Serve in the hollowed-out melon.

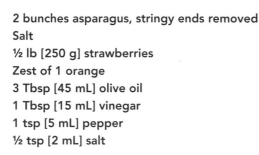

FRESH ASPARAGUS WITH STRAWBERRY VINAIGRETTE
4 TO 6 SERVINGS

A colourful splash to start a special meal.

2 bunches asparagus, stringy ends removed
Salt
½ lb [250 g] strawberries
Zest of 1 orange
3 Tbsp [45 mL] olive oil
1 Tbsp [15 mL] vinegar
1 tsp [5 mL] pepper
½ tsp [2 mL] salt

COVER THE BOTTOM of a large frying pan with water and bring to a boil. Add the asparagus, sprinkle with a little salt, cover and cook for 3 to 4 minutes. Meanwhile, in a food processor blend the strawberries with the orange zest, olive oil, vinegar, pepper and ½ tsp [2 mL] salt. Remove the asparagus from the frying pan and plunge immediately into cold water. Drain. Drizzle the sauce over the asparagus and serve.

GREENS WITH WARM PEAR AND WALNUT DRESSING
2 SERVINGS

2 handfuls baby greens or any mixed greens
1 ½ oz [42 g] blue cheese
1 pear, peeled, cored and cubed
2 Tbsp [30 mL] crushed walnuts
1 tsp [5 mL] butter
2 Tbsp [30 mL] port or wine vinegar

3 Tbsp [45 mL] olive oil
Salt and pepper

WASH THE GREENS, spin or pat them dry and place half in each of two salad bowls. Crumble the blue cheese on top. In a saucepan, sauté the pear cubes with the walnuts in the butter over medium heat until the pear cubes are lightly browned. Pour in the port. When it begins to bubble, remove the saucepan from the heat and whisk in the olive oil. Season with salt and pepper. Serve the dressing while it is still warm, over the greens and cheese.

DANDELION AND SPINACH SALAD
2 SERVINGS

Pick the dandelions from your lawn (or your neighbour's) if no chemical spray has been used on it. Otherwise, check for dandelion greens at your local market.

1 clove garlic
½ cup [125 mL] yogurt
1 Tbsp [15 mL] tahini or peanut butter
Juice of ½ lemon
1 cup [250 mL] young organic dandelion
   leaves or watercress, torn
1 cup [250 mL] fresh spinach leaves
¼ cup [50 mL] chopped nuts
   or sunflower seeds

BLEND THE GARLIC, yogurt, tahini and lemon juice in a food processor or blender until smooth. Toss with the dandelion and spinach leaves. Top with chopped nuts. Serve.

Warm (or wilted) salads don't have to be made of spinach and they don't need bacon bits. A handful of sliced fresh mushrooms warmed through in a frying pan with a dressing will make a nice little supper on rice or slices of fried bread (which the gourmets call croutons). A handful of nuts (walnuts, hazelnuts, even peanuts) tossed over medium heat for 5 minutes in a frying pan, then mixed with 2 Tbsp [30 mL] of your dressing and poured over lettuce becomes an Italian salad from Sicily—the nuts crunchy, the dressing smooth and velvety and the lettuce crisp. All it needs is sliced fresh bread.
—*Peasant's Alphabet*

> Nobody who has ever rented a tuxedo can have avoided the pretentiousness of a head waiter making a Caesar salad. And very few head waiters can have managed to avoid the timidity of somebody who says, at the last moment before serving, "Can I have mine without anchovies?" I can understand anybody's reluctance to eat a whole undecorated anchovy, but that wasn't what God had in mind when she invented them. Finely chopped in salads, gently fried with tomatoes and basil for a pasta sauce, ground into butter with a little brandy and lemon juice to put on a steak—that was what anchovies were originally meant for.
> —*Mushrooms Are Marvellous*

HOT SALAD OF SWEET PEPPERS
2 SERVINGS

You can eat this salad hot or cold with meat, fish or chicken, or make it part of a cold Mediterranean lunch the next day. The anchovies disappear—nobody can see them, but everybody will comment on the bright sweet-and-sour flavour of the sauce that sticks to the peppers.

2 or 3 shiny sweet red and yellow peppers
2 Tbsp [30 mL] olive oil
1 clove garlic, chopped
½ tsp [2 mL] salt
3 anchovy fillets
2 Tbsp [30 mL] vinegar
½ tsp [2 mL] sugar

SEED THE PEPPERS and then cut into 1-inch [2.5 cm] squares (more or less). Heat the oil in a frying pan over medium-high heat and fry the garlic for 30 seconds. Add the sweet peppers and the salt. Cook for 2 minutes, turning the peppers to coat them in oil. Add the anchovies and cook for 2 minutes, stirring so that the anchovies blend in. Add the vinegar, sprinkle with sugar and toss well for 1 minute. Serve.

CHICKPEA VINAIGRETTE
4 SERVINGS

1 small bunch parsley, chopped
2 cups [500 mL] cooked chickpeas
Juice of 1 orange
Salt and pepper

IN A BOWL, combine most of the parsley with the chickpeas, orange juice and some salt and pepper. Garnish with the remaining parsley and serve with pita bread and Tzatziki (page 24).

LENTIL SALAD
4 SERVINGS

2 cups [750 mL] water
1 cup [250 mL] dried lentils
4 Tbsp [60 mL] olive oil
Juice of ½ lemon
Zest of 1 lemon
4 green onions, chopped
1 clove garlic, chopped
1 sweet red pepper, diced
½ tsp [2 mL] pepper
½ tsp [2 mL] salt
Chopped cilantro

BRING THE WATER to a boil in a saucepan, add the lentils and simmer, covered, for 15 to 20 minutes, until the lentils are cooked but not mushy (cooking time will vary according to the variety of lentil used). Drain well. Place the lentils in a bowl and toss with the olive oil and lemon juice. Mix in the lemon zest, green onion, garlic, red pepper, pepper and salt. Garnish with cilantro and serve.

PERUVIAN POTATO SALAD

The Genius of James Barber

¼ cup [50 mL] milk
2 Tbsp [30 mL] crumbled feta cheese
2 Tbsp [30 mL] vegetable oil
2 Tbsp [30 mL] peanuts or peanut butter
½ tsp [2 mL] cayenne pepper
½ tsp [2 mL] ground black pepper
½ tsp [2 mL] salt
2 lb [1 kg] potatoes, boiled in their skins
6 hard-boiled eggs, sliced
1 tomato, sliced
1 small bunch cilantro, chopped
½ cucumber, chopped
Radishes, chopped

IN A BOWL, combine the milk, feta, oil, peanuts, cayenne pepper, black pepper and salt. Slice the potatoes thickly and lay them flat on a dish. Pour the dressing over the potatoes and garnish with the eggs, tomato, cilantro, cucumber and radishes. Serve hot, cold or warm.

THAI PAPAYA SALAD

2 SERVINGS

Wash and dry papaya seeds and use them as you would pepper.

1 small papaya
2 small red chili peppers, finely chopped
1 clove garlic, finely chopped
6 cherry tomatoes, halved
Handful of bean sprouts
Handful of roasted peanuts
1 Tbsp [15 mL] brown sugar
½ tsp [2 mL] salt
Juice of 1 lime

CUT THE PAPAYA in half, scoop out the seeds and remove the skin. Cube the flesh and combine it with the chili peppers and garlic in a bowl. Mix in the tomato halves, bean sprouts and peanuts. In a small bowl, combine the brown sugar, salt and lime juice, stirring until the sugar dissolves. Pour the dressing over the salad, toss and serve.

FRIED PRAWNS AND MANGO SALAD

4 APPETIZER OR 2 MAIN-COURSE SERVINGS

Vegetable oil
1 Tbsp [15 mL] peppercorns
1 ½ lb [750 g] whole, unpeeled prawns
2 mangoes, peeled, pitted and cubed
1 Tbsp [15 mL] grated fresh ginger
½ tsp [2 mL] salt
4 cups [1000 mL] spinach and lettuce leaves
Juice of 1 lemon
Freshly ground black pepper

HEAT ½ INCH [1 CM] VEGETABLE OIL in a heavy saucepan, add the peppercorns and heat until sizzling. Toss in the prawns and quick-fry them for 1 or 2 minutes. Drain the prawns, dry them on paper towels and combine them with the mango cubes, ginger and salt in a bowl. Place the greens on a plate and top with the mango mixture. Sprinkle with lemon juice and black pepper. Serve.

SPINACH SALAD WITH FETA AND ORANGES

4 APPETIZER OR 2 MAIN-COURSE SERVINGS

1 bunch fresh spinach, washed and drained, stems cut off
2 oranges, peeled and chopped
½ cup [125 mL] crumbled feta cheese
¼ cup [50 mL] olive oil
3 Tbsp [45 mL] wine vinegar
1 tsp [5 mL] balsamic vinegar
Salt and pepper

IN A BOWL, toss the spinach with the oranges, feta, olive oil, vinegars and some salt and pepper. Serve immediately.

HOT BACON SALAD
2 TO 4 SERVINGS

A quick, filling supper with a loaf of good bread and enough vitamins to keep scurvy at bay for a whole weekend. On its own there's lots for two, with some left over for Bubble and Squeak (page 107) the next day, and as a side dish for meat (like Barbecued Flank Steak, page 74) it's more than adequate for four. You can use spinach, cabbage or savoy cabbage sliced thin instead of lettuce, but you'll be disappointed if you use iceberg lettuce, which doesn't have enough body to give the salad its essential crispness.

8 oz [250 g] sliced bacon, cut crosswise into
   ½-inch [1 cm] lengths
1 head romaine
1 bunch green onions, cut into ½-inch [1 cm]
   lengths
2 Tbsp [30 mL] vinegar
½ tsp [2 mL] sugar
Salt and pepper

COOK BACON in a dry frying pan over medium heat for about 10 minutes, until crisp. While the bacon is frying, remove the coarse outside leaves from the romaine (keep in a plastic bag for tomorrow's soup), then cut the romaine lengthwise into quarters. Slice the quarters crosswise into 1-inch [2.5 cm] pieces, separate the leaves a bit and put them in a heatproof bowl. Remove the bacon from the pan and drain on a paper towel. Pour most of the fat from the pan (leave 3 or 4 Tbsp/45–60 mL), turn heat to high and stir-fry the green onion 1 minute. Stir in the vinegar, sugar and pepper to taste, and cook 30 seconds. Add the bacon to the greens and pour the cooked dressing over all. Toss well, add salt if needed (some bacon is saltier than others) and eat immediately with good bread and good beer.

ZUCCHINI AND MINT SALAD
4 SERVINGS

Fresh and bright, even better with butter. You can use half a dozen very small zucchini instead of one large one.

2 Tbsp [30 mL] olive oil or butter
1 large zucchini, cut into rounds
1 tsp [5 mL] salt
½ tsp [2 mL] pepper
Handful of fresh mint, chopped
Zest and juice of 1 lemon

HEAT THE OIL in a frying pan over medium heat. Add the zucchini, sprinkle with the salt and pepper and cook for 4 to 5 minutes, stirring, until tender. Garnish with the mint and lemon zest and juice. Serve warm or cold.

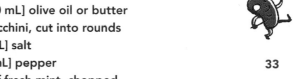

Tarragon, basil and mint are sweet herbs, and nine times out of ten they're also interchangeable. Basil has a smoothness that makes good pesto sauce, but any one of them goes very well with fish or chicken or tofu, especially if you add a splash of white wine in the last couple of minutes of your cooking. They all make a nice herbal tea (add honey to sweeten it while it's still hot, and keep it in the fridge for the next sunny afternoon). Basil goes well with chicken or fish. So does mint and so does tarragon. Each time you get something different. Nine times out of ten you'll like it, possibly even prefer it, but most of all you'll enjoy discovering something new. Slavishly following recipes is like painting by numbers: it can get very dull.
—*Cooking for Two*

Recollections of

TOM INGLIS

AIRDRIE, ALBERTA

James became part of our family legends when he mentioned on one show that it was so easy and quick to make the dish he was preparing that after you put the lid on you could just "float around looking beautiful." The way he said it was perfect and we all laughed and continue to laugh when we say it to each other (the way he did, in his accent) after finishing a task. I think what was so important to me about James was that he made cooking so accessible. You didn't need to have fancy ingredients, lots of money or a sous-chef to make his recipes. Not only was it OK to make substitutions and find low cost alternatives but he encouraged it! He seldom seemed to measure ingredients and promoted having the whole family, including children, cook together. James had a wonderful sense of humour, a love for people and good food, a passion for cooking but never seemed to take himself too seriously ... that is why he was, and still is, my culinary hero.

In a small bowl or
cup put olive oil and
salt (see below).
Green onions,carrot
sticks, sprigs raw
cauliflower, celery,
broccoli and best
of all — fennel.
JUST DIP & EAT

OLIVE OIL

SALT

SOUPS & STEWS

There are very few things that stock won't improve. Vegetables, stews, beans, lentils, rice—they all benefit from the extra flavour and extra richness that come from this enriched liquid. And the making of stock is ridiculously easy because it makes itself while you do something else. Stock cubes are a last resort. A lot of restaurants have a stockpot on a low flame all night—nobody watches it, nobody worries. You can do exactly the same, or you can let it simmer while you go to a movie, watch the box, make love or sweep the dust balls from under the bed. Saturday afternoons in winter are my favourite times for making stock—everybody else is skiing or getting cold standing around garage sales, but we've got feet up, books to read, tea and chocolate biscuits while the stockpot quietly bubbles. Water, bones, onions and carrots are the basics for stock. There is no single recipe, although you'll find all kinds of cookbooks insisting not only that you roast the bones but that you only use bones from pedigreed animals of superior intelligence. Ignore them. Restaurants make stock that way, but restaurants have people to clean their ovens and scrub their pans.
—*Cooking for Two*

BASIC CHICKEN STOCK
MAKES ABOUT 6 CUPS [1.5 L]

Every time I make chicken I freeze the leftover bones and skin until I need to make stock. I do that with onion skins, too, and the butt ends of carrots and leeks. If you don't have 2 onion skins for this soup, it will be delicious with just the leek.

1 chicken carcass or 1 lb [500 g] leftover
   chicken bones
1 large carrot
1 leek
1 stalk celery or 1 Tbsp [15 mL] celery salt
1 bay leaf
1 Tbsp [15 mL] peppercorns
Skin of 2 onions
Handful of parsley
Water

PLACE THE CHICKEN carcass, carrot, leek, celery, bay leaf, peppercorns, onion skins and parsley in a large pot (the bigger the better) and fill the pot with enough water to cover the chicken carcass by a few inches. Bring to a rolling boil over medium heat, and use a spoon to remove any scum that may be produced. Reduce the heat to as low as possible and simmer the stock overnight, or keep the heat at medium and allow the stock to cook for 3 hours or so, until it has a nice yellow colour. Pour the stock through a fine strainer into small containers for freezing. If you like your stock strong, cook the reduced stock over medium heat for another 40 minutes or so.

AVGOLEMONO FOR TWO
Break 1 egg into a bowl and beat with a fork. Beat in the juice of 1 lemon and pour hot Basic Chicken Stock into the mixture 1 tsp [5 mL] at a time until the egg mixture is warm. Add the egg mixture to 2 cups of hot stock and add ½ cup [125 mL] cooked rice. Heat through (but don't boil) and serve, sprinkled with chopped parsley. —*Quick and Simple*

CREAM OF MANGO SOUP
2 SERVINGS

2 to 3 slices fresh ginger, finely chopped, or
    1 tsp [5 mL] powdered ginger
1 can mango or 1 fresh mango, peeled,
    pitted and chopped
1 cup [250 mL] yogurt
½ tsp [2 mL] salt
Juice of ½ lemon
1 tsp [5 mL] toasted cumin seeds
Chopped basil or cilantro

PLACE THE GINGER, mango, yogurt, salt and lemon juice in a food processor or blender and process until smooth. Serve cold, sprinkled with cumin seeds and basil.

COLD CARROT, GINGER AND LIME SOUP
4 SERVINGS

This soup is also delicious when served hot. You can replace the buttermilk with 1 cup [250 mL] milk mixed with the juice of 1 lime.

2 Tbsp [30 mL] vegetable oil
4 large carrots, grated
½-inch [1 cm] piece fresh ginger, grated
1 cup [250 mL] chicken stock
1 small green chili pepper, chopped
1 cup [250 mL] buttermilk
Juice of 2 limes
Salt and pepper

HEAT THE OIL in a saucepan over medium-high heat. Add the carrots and ginger, and cook for 2 minutes, or until the carrots start to caramelize. Stir in the stock, and bring the mixture to a boil. Reduce the heat to low and cook for 7 to 8 minutes, until the carrots are tender. Stir in the chili pepper, buttermilk and lime juice. Purée the carrot mixture in a food processor or with a hand-held blender. Season with salt and pepper. Chill the soup before serving.

TURKISH PARSLEY SOUP
2 SERVINGS

If you want to serve this as a dip, thicken it by adding another slice of bread. Serve soup or dip with more baguette.

3 cloves garlic, chopped
1 cucumber, chopped
1 thick slice French bread
1 cup [250 mL] yogurt
½ cup [125 mL] walnuts
2 Tbsp [30 mL] olive oil
Handful of parsley
Salt and pepper

COMBINE THE GARLIC, cucumber, bread, yogurt, walnuts, oil, parsley and some salt and pepper in a food processor, blending until smooth. If you prefer a thinner consistency, throw some ice cubes into the processor and blend again. Serve cold.

RED WINE AND RED ONION SOUP
6 SERVINGS

2 Tbsp [30 mL] butter
4 red onions, finely chopped
3 cloves garlic, finely chopped
Sprig of thyme, chopped or 2 tsp [10 mL]
    dried
2 tomatoes, chopped
6 cups [1.5 L] stock
1 cup [250 mL] red wine
Salt and pepper

HEAT THE BUTTER in a large pot over high heat, Add the onion, garlic and thyme, and cook for 2 to 3 minutes, until the onion is tender. Add the tomato and cook for 1 minute. Pour in the stock and wine, bring to a boil, reduce the heat and simmer for 10 minutes. Season with salt and pepper, and serve.

SWEET PEPPER SOUP

2 Tbsp [30 mL] olive oil
1 onion, chopped
2 tomatoes, chopped
1 sweet red pepper, chopped
1 cup [250 mL] apple juice
½ tsp [2 mL] powdered ginger
Juice of 1 lemon
Salt and pepper

HEAT THE OIL in a frying pan and fry the onion until transparent. Stir in the tomatoes and pepper, apple juice, ginger, lemon juice and some salt and pepper. Cover and simmer for 20 to 25 minutes. Purée the mixture in a blender or food processor. Serve.

BEER SOUP

2 Tbsp [30 mL] olive oil
3 to 4 cloves garlic, chopped
1 onion, finely chopped
Large hunk of stale bread
1 bottle beer
1 cup [250 mL] hot water
1 tsp [5 mL] caraway seeds
½ tsp [2 mL] dried oregano
½ tsp [2 mL] salt
Freshly ground pepper
Strips of sweet red pepper

HEAT THE OIL in a saucepan over medium heat and sauté the garlic and onion. Tear the bread into small pieces and add to the pan. Stir well. When the bread has soaked up all the juices, add the beer, water, caraway seeds, oregano, salt and some pepper. Cover and simmer for 10 to 15 minutes over moderate heat. Serve garnished with strips of red pepper.

PAPPA AL POMODORO

You don't need stock for this soup—the bread gives it the flavour. The ginger isn't traditional, so leave it out if you prefer.

2 medium onions, finely chopped
5 thin slices fresh ginger (optional)
1 Tbsp [15 mL] olive oil
16 oz [500 mL] canned crushed tomatoes
Dollop of tomato paste
Small glass wine
Water
2 slices good bread
Salt

IN A LARGE SAUCEPAN, fry the onion and ginger (if using) in the olive oil for 5 minutes. Add the crushed tomato and bring to a boil. Add a dollop of tomato paste and pour in the wine and 4 wine glasses of water. Bring to a boil. Tear up the bread and add it to the pan, along with some salt. Cover and cook for 15 minutes. Stir to break up the bread completely. Adjust the salt to taste and serve.

Soups & Stews

BEET BORSCHT

2 SERVINGS

1 tsp [5 mL] butter
1 cup [250 mL] boiled beets, chopped,
    or 1 medium can beets
1 tsp [5 mL] chopped dill
1 clove garlic, chopped
1 Tbsp [15 mL] chopped parsley
Water or chicken stock
Juice of 1 orange
4 pearl onions, peeled
½ tsp [2 mL] salt
2 Tbsp [30 mL] yogurt or sour cream

MELT THE BUTTER in a saucepan over medium heat. Stir in the beets, dill, garlic and parsley, and add enough water to cover the beets. Pour in the orange juice and add the pearl onions and salt. Cook over medium heat for about 10 to 15 minutes. Stir in the yogurt and serve.

TOMATO, GIN AND GINGER SOUP

2 SERVINGS

A big hotel classic—fresh, bright, smooth and easy.

2 Tbsp [30 mL] butter
3 green onions, chopped
2 tomatoes, chopped
2-inch [5 cm] piece fresh ginger, chopped
1 tsp [5 mL] salt
1 tsp [5 mL] pepper
2 cups [500 mL] water
¾ cup [175 mL] cream
3 Tbsp [45 mL] gin
Handful of parsley, chopped

MELT THE BUTTER in a saucepan over medium heat. Add the green onion and tomato, and cook for 2 to 3 minutes. Add the ginger, salt and pepper, and cook for 2 minutes. Transfer the tomato mixture to a food processor and process until smooth. Return the soup to the saucepan, add the water and bring to a boil. Remove the soup from the heat, and stir in the cream, gin and parsley. Serve.

SOPA DE TORTILLA

4 SERVINGS

Mexico in a bowl.

1 Tbsp [30 mL] vegetable oil
4 cloves garlic, chopped
1 jalapeño pepper, chopped
½ onion, chopped
2 tomatoes, chopped
4 cups [1 L] stock
Handful of cilantro, chopped
Pinch of salt
Handful of tortilla chips
Shredded cheddar cheese
Juice of 1 lime

HEAT THE OIL in a frying pan over high heat and cook the garlic, jalapeño and onion until softened. Transfer to a food processor and combine with the tomato, stock, most of the cilantro (reserve some for garnish) and a little salt. Blend until smooth. Place the mixture in a saucepan and bring to a boil. To serve, put some tortilla chips in the bottom of the soup bowls and pour the soup over top. Sprinkle on some shredded cheddar, a squeeze of lime juice and the remaining cilantro.

POOR MAN'S HOT AND SOUR SOUP

`4 SERVINGS`

If you like this type of soup really sour, just add more vinegar.

4 cups [1 L] water or stock
3 chilis
1 boneless skinless chicken breast, chopped
1 clove garlic, chopped
½ sweet red pepper, chopped
½ pkg [500 g pkg] medium tofu, cut into
    bite-sized pieces
4 mushrooms, sliced
1 onion, chopped
1-inch [2.5 cm] piece fresh ginger, grated
2 Tbsp [30 mL] soy sauce
2 Tbsp [30 mL] cornstarch
6 Tbsp [90 mL] vinegar
2 green onions, finely chopped

BRING THE WATER to a boil and add the chilis, chicken, garlic, red pepper and tofu. Return to a boil and add the mushrooms, onion, ginger and soy sauce. Simmer for 5 minutes. In a small bowl, mix the cornstarch with the vinegar. Pour the mixture into the soup and bring the soup to a boil again. Serve sprinkled with green onion.

BLACK BEAN AND BANANA SOUP

`6 SERVINGS`

Soul food in 15 minutes.

2 Tbsp [30 mL] vegetable oil
2 cloves garlic, chopped
1 onion, chopped
2 Tbsp [30 mL] chopped oregano
2 tsp [10 mL] cumin
2 chilis, chopped
2 tomatoes, chopped
2 bananas, peeled and chopped
2 cans [each 14 oz/398 mL] black beans,
    rinsed and drained
½ cup [125 mL] stock or water

Handful of cilantro, chopped
Salt and pepper

HEAT THE OIL in a large pot over high heat. Add the garlic, onion, oregano and cumin. Cook for 2 to 3 minutes, and then add the chilis, tomato and half the banana. Cook for 2 minutes. Stir in the black beans, stock and most of the cilantro (reserve some for garnish), bring to a boil, reduce the heat to medium and cook for 10 more minutes. For a chunky soup, leave it just as it is; for a smooth soup, purée the mixture in a food processor or blender. Season with salt and pepper, and serve with the remaining chopped banana and cilantro sprinkled over top.

Soups & Stews

CREAM OF CHICKPEA SOUP

`4 SERVINGS`

A real belly warmer.

2 Tbsp [30 mL] vegetable oil
3 cloves garlic, chopped
1 carrot, chopped
1 chili
1 onion, chopped
1 can [19 oz/540 g] chickpeas, rinsed and
    drained
4 cups [1 L] stock
½ tsp [2 mL] cumin
Bunch of parsley, chopped
Sprig of oregano, chopped, or 1 tsp [5 mL]
    dried
½ cup [125 mL] yogurt
Salt and pepper

HEAT THE OIL in a pot over high heat. Add the garlic, carrot, chili and onion. Cook for 2 minutes. Add the chickpeas, stock, cumin, most of the parsley (reserve some for garnish) and oregano. Bring to a boil, reduce the heat and simmer for 10 minutes. Transfer the soup to a food processor and blend until smooth. Stir in the yogurt and season with salt and pepper. Sprinkle with the remaining parsley and serve.

DAL

This lentil dish is great to eat with roti, an Indian flatbread, or tortillas if you can't find roti. It goes well with basmati rice, too.

1 cup [250 mL] small orange lentils
2 cups [500 mL] water
2 Tbsp [30 mL] vegetable oil
6 slices ginger
3 cloves garlic, finely chopped
1 onion, finely chopped
½ cup [125 mL] grated coconut
1 tsp [5 mL] curry powder
1 tsp [5 mL] pepper
½ tsp [2 mL] cayenne pepper or hot pepper flakes
1 cup [250 mL] yogurt
½ tsp [2 mL] salt
Juice of 1 lemon
Chopped cilantro
Grated coconut

PLACE THE LENTILS and water in a saucepan and cook over medium heat for 15 to 20 minutes. Heat the oil in a frying pan and fry the ginger, garlic and onion until the onion has browned. Stir in the coconut, curry powder, pepper and cayenne. Add the cooked lentils, and stir in the yogurt, salt and lemon juice. Cook for a further 2 to 3 minutes. Remove the pieces of ginger. Serve garnished with cilantro and coconut.

CORN AND BLACK BEAN CHILI

6 SERVINGS

"Macho" doesn't always mean meat.

2 Tbsp [30 mL] vegetable oil
4 cloves garlic, chopped
1 onion, chopped
2 chilis, chopped
1 can [14 oz/398 mL] black beans, rinsed and drained

1 can [14 oz/398 mL] tomatoes or 3 fresh chopped
2 cups [500 mL] stock or water
½ cup [125 mL] barley or rice
1 Tbsp [15 mL] chili powder
1 tsp [5 mL] cumin
1 tsp [5 mL] dried oregano
1 sweet red pepper, diced
1 sweet green pepper, diced
1 cup [250 mL] corn kernels, canned, fresh or frozen
Salt and pepper
2 green onions, thinly sliced
Sour cream

HEAT THE OIL in a large pot over high heat. Add the garlic and onion, and cook for 2 minutes. Add the chilis, beans, tomato, stock, barley, chili powder, cumin and oregano. Bring to a boil and cook, covered, for 15 minutes. Toss in the peppers and corn, and cook a further 5 minutes. Season with salt and pepper. Serve sprinkled with green onion and with some sour cream on the side

MUSHROOM AND MUSSEL RAGOÛT

4 SERVINGS

Fresh mussels, fresh mushrooms and that's about it.

1 Tbsp [15 mL] butter
2 cloves garlic, chopped
1 onion, chopped
2 lb [1 kg] fresh mussels, scrubbed
1 cup [250 mL] sliced mushrooms
1 cup [250 mL] water
1 glass white wine
½ tsp [2 mL] thyme
Salt and pepper
2 Tbsp [30 mL] cream
2 Tbsp [30 mL] chopped parsley

MELT THE BUTTER over medium heat in a large pot. Add the garlic and onion. Cook for 2 minutes, and then add the mussels, mushrooms, water, wine, thyme and some salt and pepper. Turn the heat up to high, bring the mixture to a boil, cover and let cook for 4 to 5 minutes, until the mussels have opened and the mushrooms are tender. Discard any mussels that remain closed. Stir in the cream. Serve the ragoût with parsley sprinkled over top.

CLAM CHOWDER
4 SERVINGS

5 to 6 slices bacon, chopped
4 to 5 slices fresh ginger
3 tomatoes, chopped
2 cloves garlic, chopped
2 potatoes, diced
2 stalks celery, chopped
1 onion, chopped
1 Tbsp [15 mL] chopped parsley
1 bay leaf
Freshly ground pepper
2 lb [1 kg] fresh clams, scrubbed, or 2 cans clams
1 tsp [5 mL] dill
Cherry tomatoes, halved

FRY THE BACON in a large saucepan over high heat. Add the ginger, chopped tomato, garlic, potato, celery, onion, parsley, bay leaf and some pepper. Stir well. If using canned clams, strain the juice from the clams and add it to the saucepan, reserving the clams. Cover the saucepan and simmer for 10 to 15 minutes, adding more liquid if necessary. Toss in the clams, dill, and cherry tomatoes about 5 to 10 minutes before serving and heat through.

OYSTER AND ARTICHOKE SOUP
2 SERVINGS

This soup would be an exotic opening to an elegant entrée.

2 Tbsp [30 mL] butter
3 green onions, chopped (separate white and green parts)
½ lb [250 g] shucked fresh oysters

1 can [14 oz/398 mL] artichoke hearts, drained and quartered
1 cup [250 mL] whipping cream
1 glass white wine or de-alcoholized white wine
Chopped parsley
Salt and pepper

MELT THE BUTTER in a saucepan. Add white part of the onions, and sauté for 2 to 3 minutes. Toss in the oysters and cook for 2 to 3 minutes. Add the artichoke hearts, cream, wine and parsley, and sprinkle on a little salt and pepper. Bring to a boil. Serve garnished with the green part of the onions.

CARIBBEAN CABBAGE SOUP
6 SERVINGS

You can use either fresh or powdered ginger in this soup. Garnish it with chopped green onion or cilantro.

1 cup [250 mL] white wine
1 cup [250 mL] dried shrimp
2 Tbsp [30 mL] vegetable oil
3 slices fresh ginger, finely chopped, or ½ tsp [2 mL] powdered ginger
1 medium onion, chopped
1 large potato, skin on, washed and diced
½ tsp [2 mL] cayenne pepper
½ tsp [2 mL] salt
6 cups [1.5 L] hot water
½ green cabbage, quartered, cored and sliced
1 tsp [5 mL] black pepper
¼ cup [50 mL] grated coconut
Juice and zest of ½ lemon
½ lb [250 g] fresh shrimp, peeled, deveined and rinsed

PLACE THE WHITE wine in a bowl, add the dried shrimp and let stand for 30 minutes. Heat the oil in a frying pan over medium heat and fry the ginger and onion for 1 minute. Add the potato and toss until glistening. Stir in the cayenne and salt, and toss well until potato is lightly browned. Add the dried shrimp and wine, hot water, cabbage and black pepper, and simmer the mixture for 5 to 10 minutes, until cabbage is tender. Add the coconut, lemon juice and zest and the fresh shrimp and continue to cook for 1 minute or until shrimp is pink and curled. Serve immediately.

LAKSA

8 oz [250 g] dried Chinese noodles
2 Tbsp [30 mL] vegetable oil
2 cloves garlic, chopped
2 small red chili peppers, chopped
1-inch [2.5 cm] piece fresh ginger, chopped
12 fresh prawns, peeled, deveined and rinsed
1 can [14 oz/398 mL] coconut milk
2 cups [500 mL] water
1 tsp [5 mL] salt
½ tsp [2 mL] turmeric
Handful of bean sprouts
Handful of cilantro, chopped

PUT A LARGE POT of water on to boil. Cook the noodles in the boiling water until they are tender. Drain them and place them in a pot of cool water while you prepare the laksa. Heat the oil in a wok over high heat. Add the garlic, chili peppers and ginger, and cook for 1 minute, stirring constantly. Toss in the prawns, and reduce the heat to medium. Immediately add the coconut milk, water, salt and turmeric. Bring the mixture to a boil. Drain the noodles, and divide them between two bowls. Pour the laksa over top, and serve sprinkled with bean sprouts and cilantro.

MATELOTE DE FÉVRIER, OR MY AUNT SALLIE'S CHEAPO 20-MINUTE BOUILLABAISSE

Eat this hearty chowder with bread and gusto.

2 Tbsp [30 mL] butter
2 cloves garlic, finely chopped
1 medium onion, coarsely chopped
7 oz/200 mL canned crushed tomatoes or 2 ripe tomatoes, chopped
1 lb [500 g] mushrooms, halved
2 Tbsp [30 mL] canned anchovies or Asian fish sauce
1 cup [250 mL] apple juice, white wine or beer
1 tsp [5 mL] crushed thyme
2 lb [1 kg] white fish cut into 1½-inch [4 cm] pieces
1 oz [30 mL] rye whiskey
½ cup [125 mL] plain yogurt or sour cream
2 Tbsp [30 mL] soy sauce

HEAT THE BUTTER in a frying pan over low heat. Add the garlic and onion, cover and cook for 5 minutes. Stir in the tomatoes, mushrooms, anchovies, apple juice and thyme, and simmer, uncovered, for 10 minutes. Add the fish, pushing the pieces into the sauce. Increase the heat to high and bring the fish mixture to a boil. Then lower the heat, cover and simmer for 6 minutes. Stir in the whiskey and cook for 1 minute. Stir in the yogurt and soy sauce and heat briefly.

TURKEY SOUP WITH CHILIED WALNUTS

2 SERVINGS

The spiced walnuts are a wonderful garnish for this soup.

SOUP

1 Tbsp [15 mL] butter or vegetable oil
3 slices of fresh ginger, julienned
1 onion, chopped
1 tomato, chopped
2 cups [500 mL] cider (1 bottle)
About 1 cup [250 mL] cooked cubed turkey
1 tsp [5 mL] finely chopped orange zest
1 tsp [5 mL] thyme, sage or oregano
Salt and pepper
About 1 tsp [5 mL] soy sauce

HEAT THE BUTTER in a saucepan over medium heat and fry the ginger and onion until soft. Add the tomato, cider, turkey, orange zest, thyme and some salt and pepper, cover and simmer for 20 minutes. Stir in the soy sauce (adjust to taste) and simmer a few minutes longer.

CHILIED WALNUTS

1 clove garlic, crushed
½ cup [125 mL] walnut pieces
½ tsp [2 mL] cayenne pepper
½ tsp [2 mL] salt
2 Tbsp [30 mL] vegetable oil or butter

PLACE THE GARLIC, walnuts, cayenne and salt in a paper bag and shake well. Heat the oil in a frying pan over low heat and sauté the nuts for about a minute, until garlic is lightly browned. Remove the nuts and let cool on a paper towel. Serve as a garnish for turkey soup.

MUSHROOM, LEEK AND POTATO SOUP
`4 SERVINGS`

Potatoes, leeks and mushrooms go together naturally. This soup is quick and easy, a very filling and nourishing dish that, given a little more fussing (such as putting it through the blender or adding a little cream at the end), would finish up with a very fancy French name—vichyssoise. I prefer it a little chunky, served with big hunks of rye bread. If you want to make lots of it for an après-ski party, just double, treble or even quadruple everything.

3 slices fat bacon, chopped
1 medium onion, chopped
1 large leek, thinly sliced
1 large potato, finely diced
½ lb [250 g] fresh mushrooms, chopped
1 tsp [5 mL] salt
½ tsp [2 mL] pepper
3 cups [750 mL] water
½ tsp [2 mL] grated nutmeg

IN A LARGE heavy pot, fry the bacon over medium heat until the fat starts to flow. Add the onion and fry. Toss in the leek and stir to coat it well with bacon fat. Continue to cook over medium heat, until leek is soft but not brown. Add the potato, mushrooms, salt and pepper, and stir well. Pour in the water and bring to a boil. Simmer for 20 minutes. Stir in the nutmeg and serve the soup immediately.

A NICE LAMB STEW FOR THE MIDDLE OF WINTER
`2 SERVINGS`

2 Tbsp [30 mL] vegetable oil
8 oz [250 g] stewing lamb, cut into
    bite-sized pieces
3 tomatoes, chopped
2 or 3 sage leaves, chopped
2 cloves garlic, chopped
1 small onion, chopped
1 can [19 oz/540 mL] brown lentils,
    rinsed and drained
2 cups [500 mL] water
Salt and pepper

PREHEAT OVEN TO 350F [180C]. Heat the oil in an ovenproof pot over medium-high heat. Add the lamb and cook for 3 minutes, or until it is browned on all sides. Add the tomatoes, sage, garlic, onion, lentils, water and some salt and pepper to the pot, and stir. Cover the pot and put it in the oven. Cook for 90 minutes, or until the lamb is tender and the lentils have absorbed most of the water (check the pot every half-hour to make sure the stew doesn't get too dry—if it does, just add another cup of water).

Spring is a time of surprises, but, like birthday presents, not all of them are welcome. Cold winds and runny noses, summer in the morning and winter at night. And rain, more times than sometimes. Wet and cold and calculatingly relentless rain. It runs down windows, it soaks into shoes and it takes the crease out of pants and destroys hundred-dollar hairdos. Cops, hookers, people who walk to work and night-hunting cats all think twice when they are wet. Rain has not pity for the urban peasants; it locks them in behind their doors with the nineteen-inch screen for friendship and pizza for supper.

Spring is a time for comfort, and there is no comfort like a stew in springtime. Beef stew, pork stew, chicken stew and Irish stew; the cookbooks are full of stews, but very few people make them today. Stews take time, that long, slow, meditative and comforting cooking time that is really the main and most important ingredient. —*Peasant's Alphabet*

BŒUF BOURGUIGNON
6 TO 8 SERVINGS

Cooking a large stew takes no longer than cooking a small one, and there is no simpler, more welcoming way to feed half a dozen friends than stewing a good piece of beef in the Bourgogne style. Most stew recipes call for cut-up meat, but this one uses a small boneless rump roast that arrives at the table with no little splendour, surrounded by mushrooms and small onions, further reinforcing your reputation for cleverness in the kitchen. Of course, you'll have to slice the meat, but you'll have avoided serving plain old stew.

MARINADE
1 boneless rump roast [4–5 lb/2–2.5 kg]
1 medium onion, chopped
2 cloves garlic, chopped
2 tsp [10 mL] thyme
1 tsp [5 mL] salt
½ tsp [2 mL] pepper
1 bay leaf
2 Tbsp [30 mL] vegetable oil
1 bottle dry red wine

WITH A SKEWER, poke a few dozen deep holes in the roast. Lay half the chopped onion, half the garlic, half the thyme, and the salt, pepper and bay leaf in the bottom of an earthenware, glass or enamelled pot just big enough to hold the roast. Place the roast on the vegetables, spread the remaining onion, garlic and thyme over it and drizzle it with the oil. Carefully pour the wine down the side, to cover the meat. Leave the roast to marinate in a cool place or the refrigerator for 24 hours, covered and undisturbed.

SAUCE
3 Tbsp [45 mL] vegetable oil
5 Tbsp [75 mL] butter
1 lb [500 g] fresh mushrooms, whole caps
  and chopped stalks
½ lb [250 g] lean bacon or ham, chopped
1 ½ tsp [7 mL] all-purpose flour
2 cups [500 mL] water or stock
1 tsp [5 mL] crushed rosemary
24 small onions

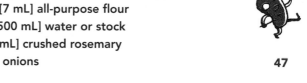

FOUR HOURS BEFORE dinner, remove the meat from the marinade, reserving the marinade. Dry the meat well. In a stew pot, heat the oil over high heat and brown the meat all over, turning it with tongs. Remove the meat and pour off the oil. Melt 3 Tbsp [45 mL] of the butter in the pot over medium heat and fry mushroom stalks and bacon for 2 to 3 minutes. Add the flour, stir well and cook for another 2 to 3 minutes. Slowly add the water and then the reserved marinade and the rosemary. Bring to a boil, return the meat to the pot and cover tightly. Cook either on top of the stove at the very lowest heat, barely simmering, for 4 hours, or in the oven at 225F (105C) for the same time.

Fifteen minutes before serving, peel the onions. (Run them under hot water for 5 minutes; the skins will then slip off easily.) In a frying pan over medium heat, lightly brown the onions in the remaining butter. Remove them from the pan, add the mushroom caps and cook for 4 minutes. Remove the meat from the pot, strain the sauce into a bowl, wipe the pot and return the meat to it. Add the mushroom caps, onions and sauce, and simmer for 10 minutes. Place the meat on a platter, pile the mushrooms and onions around it, pour some of the sauce over it all and serve the remainder on the side.

BEEF AND GUINNESS STEW
2 SERVINGS

If you haven't got Guinness, any other stout or dark beer will do.

2 Tbsp [30 mL] all-purpose flour
1 lb [500 g] stewing beef, cut into bite-sized
   pieces
2 Tbsp [30 mL] butter
2 carrots, chopped
1 onion, chopped
1 bay leaf
1 bottle Guinness stout
1 cup [250 mL] beef stock
Salt and pepper

PLACE THE FLOUR in a small bowl and dredge the beef pieces in the flour. Melt the butter in a pot over medium heat. Add the beef and cook until it changes colour, about 5 minutes. Add the carrot, onion and bay leaf, and cook for 3 minutes. Stir in the stout and stock, and bring to a boil. Reduce the heat and simmer for 30 minutes, until the stew has thickened slightly. Season with salt and pepper, remove bay leaf and serve.

UGLY VEGETABLE AND SAUSAGE STEW
2 SERVINGS

2 Italian sausages, sliced
2 Tbsp [30 mL] vegetable oil
1 onion, chopped
½ rutabaga, peeled and grated
1 carrot, grated
1 potato, peeled and grated
4 cups [1 L] stock
A sprig of fresh thyme or ½ tsp [2 mL] dried
Salt and pepper

PLACE THE SAUSAGE slices in a frying pan and cook until browned on both sides. Remove from heat and set aside. Heat the oil in a large pot over high heat. Add the onion, rutabaga, carrot and potato, and cook for 3 to 4 minutes, until the onion starts to caramelize. Add the stock and thyme, bring to a boil and let cook for about 10 minutes, until the vegetables are tender. Season and stir in the sausage.

POULTRY & MEAT

FRENCH-STYLE CHICKEN LIVERS
`2 SERVINGS`

In France they use duck livers and some very fancy booze called Armagnac. We don't have very much of either, so I reworked this recipe into standard super-market ingredients. Which, of course, is the only way to cook. Use what's handy and do your best.

This is a ridiculously simple dish that can stand up against anybody's pretensions of haute cuisine. It is quite wonderful when cherries are used instead of grapes, and if you want to be really imaginative you can whiz it through the blender, put it in little bowls, chill it for an hour or so and serve it as a mousse. All good things are simpler than we think.

½ lb [250 g] chicken livers
2 Tbsp [30 mL] brandy
1 Tbsp [15 mL] grainy mustard
1 Tbsp [15 mL] soy sauce
Green and black grapes
Cabbage or lettuce leaf

HEAT UP A SAUCEPAN and put the chicken livers into the hot, dry pan. Stir in the brandy, mustard and soy sauce; cover and cook over low heat for 2 to 3 minutes.

Add a good handful of green and black grapes, cook for 1 minute and serve on the cabbage leaf.

CHICKEN THAI-STYLE
`2 SERVINGS`

4 Tbsp [60 mL] coconut milk, stirred
6 to 8 whole dried chilies
2 cloves garlic, finely chopped
1 to 2 slices fresh ginger, julienned
½ onion, chopped
Zest and juice of 1 lime or lemon
1 whole boneless skinless chicken breast, cut into bite-sized pieces
1 small bunch asparagus, cut diagonally
Chopped cilantro

HEAT THE COCONUT MILK in a frying pan over medium heat. Add the chilies, garlic, ginger, onion and 1 Tbsp [15 mL] lime zest. Stir well and cook until the onion is transparent. Add the chicken pieces and cook for 5 to 6 minutes. Toss in the asparagus, and cover and cook for 2 minutes. Pour in the lime juice, stir to combine and serve the chicken garnished with cilantro.

CHICKEN WITH PEANUTS

2 SERVINGS

This is a reputation maker that takes 20 minutes to prepare and is better than any takeout. Make this dish first with peanuts. Then try almonds or cashews, even walnuts. Coconuts are not recommended unless you're cooking an ostrich. Serve it with rice.

1 whole boneless skinless chicken breast or 4
    deboned thighs
1 tsp [5 mL] cornstarch
1 tsp [5 mL] red pepper flakes
2 Tbsp [30 mL] olive oil
1 medium onion, coarsely chopped
½ cup [250 mL] dry-roasted or salted
    peanuts
2 Tbsp [30 mL] soy sauce
2 Tbsp [30 mL] whiskey (or whatever you've got)
¼ cup [50 mL] water

CUT THE CHICKEN into bite-sized pieces and toss in a bowl with the cornstarch and pepper flakes. Heat the oil in a frying pan over medium heat and cook the chicken for 1 minute. Turn and cook for 1 minute more. Add the onion and cook for 2 minutes. Toss in the peanuts and cook for 3 minutes. Pour in the soy sauce and whiskey, and cook for 1 minute. Add the water, stir well and cook for 3 to 4 minutes. Serve with rice.

CHICKEN WITH ORANGES AND BROCCOLI

2 SERVINGS

Honest, simple, colourful, light, nourishing, different, easy, quick. This is a refinement of Poulet à l'orange. It's simpler and much better. If you want to fancy it up, add a little sherry with the orange juice, or grate a little fresh ginger into the pan at the start.

1 Tbsp [15 mL] butter
1 Tbsp [15 mL] vegetable oil
3-inch [7.5 cm] piece fresh ginger, julienned
1 skinless chicken breast, halved

2 oranges, peeled and segmented
Freshly ground pepper
6 whole mushrooms
1 tsp [5 mL] dried thyme
1 small head broccoli, broken into florets
Salt

HEAT THE BUTTER and oil in a frying pan over medium heat. Add the ginger and then the chicken. When the chicken begins to show white around the edges, turn it and add the orange segments and some pepper. Toss in the whole mushrooms and the thyme, place the broccoli florets on top and season with salt. Cover and simmer for 10 to 15 minutes. Serve.

COQ AU BEER

2 SERVINGS

Perhaps it should be called Coq à la bière, but we're not being strictly French about this; we're making country food—a mellow, rich and simple dinner the like of which I've enjoyed in France and Belgium and Holland, in Denmark and in Poland. Anywhere that people brew beer and eat chicken you'll find variations of this dish because that's the way real cooking develops—not from a complicated foreign recipe, but from whatever's at hand half an hour before dinner time.

2 slices bacon, chopped
4 chicken thighs
3 carrots, chopped
1 onion, chopped
1 tsp [5 mL] dried thyme
Bay leaf
Freshly ground pepper
1 bottle beer
½ tsp [2 mL] salt
Chopped parsley

SAUTÉ THE BACON in a frying pan over high heat for a few minutes. Add the chicken thighs, skin side down, and brown them on both sides. Add the carrot, onion, thyme, bay leaf and some pepper. Stir

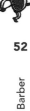

The Genius of James Barber

well. Pour in the beer; cover and simmer on low heat for about 30 minutes, adding the salt toward the end of the cooking time. Remove the bay leaf. Garnish the chicken with the parsley and serve.

EIGHT-LEGGED CHICKEN
8 SERVINGS

You have to prepare this early, before the guests arrive. Don't drink too much while you're doing it or it will look like a low-budget horror movie; and try to get someone to help you, because a secret shared is containable. People think you're crazy if you walk around alone for an hour smiling that secret smirk, but if there are two of you smiling they just think you're over-reacting to sex in the afternoon.

BUY A CHICKEN and 6 extra legs. Stitch the extra legs onto the chicken using cotton thread. Stuff the chicken with some chopped lemons and a handful of garlic and rub all over with salt. Roast in a 400F [200C] oven, basting every 15 minutes, for 20 minutes per pound. Serve to astounded guests!

EIGHT-HOUR CHICKEN WITH SAUCE SUPRÈME
4 TO 6 SERVINGS

The most successful meal I have ever cooked this way was one evening or early morning when I came home drunk, got into bed and remembered I had guests coming for lunch. I crawled out of bed, pulled the chicken out of the fridge, and managed, at the third attempt, to get it into the frying pan. And the frying pan, at the fourth attempt, into the oven. There it lay until my guests woke me the next day. They were very smug but not as smug as I when, 20 minutes after they

arrived, they were sitting down to roast chicken.

Try it with cheap frozen lamb rubbed with oregano and garlic. Get a cheap roast of pork and treat it to lots of basil and a little pepper and salt. Get a cross rib roast, and massage it with garlic and pepper and salt. Get an old duck, or a real monster of an old goose that has to be cheap; poke an onion or two inside and maybe an orange. Forget it. Don't worry. Write a book. Teach yourself to crochet. Join Men's Lib. But forget the dinner until you are ready to eat. Serve it with rice, which will cook in the time it takes to make the sauce.

1 roasting chicken or fryer, as big as you like
2 Tbsp [30 mL] butter
2 tsp [10 mL] salt
1 tsp [5 mL] pepper
1 medium onion, finely chopped
½ cup [125 mL] white wine (red wine or
    vermouth will do in a pinch)
1 tsp [5 mL] tarragon
½ lb [250 g] mushrooms, small or quartered
½ cup [125 mL] whipping cream

PREHEAT OVEN TO 180F [80C]. Massage the chicken well with the butter, salt and pepper. Crinkle a sheet of foil, straighten it out and place it in a big frying pan or a flattish baking dish. Put the chicken on the foil and lay another crinkled and straightened piece of foil loosely over the top; just lay it over, don't tuck it in. Put the pan in oven and forget it for at least 5 hours and at most 8 hours. You can go shopping, work on that great screenplay or just sleep if it's been that kind of week.

After 5 to 8 hours, remove the chicken from the oven. Put the chicken on a plate and cover with foil to keep it warm. Pour the juices from the bottom piece of foil back into the pan. Add the onion, wine and tarragon, and cook over high heat for 5 minutes. Toss in the mushrooms, cook for 4 minutes and pour in the cream. Cook for 1 minute, and there's your Sauce Suprème. Serve the chicken immediately with lots of sauce and rice.

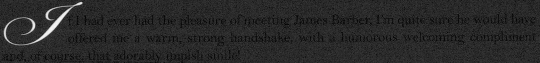

JILL GOWARD
COOKBOOK AUTHOR

54

Jill Goward

If I had ever had the pleasure of meeting James Barber, I'm quite sure he would have offered me a warm, strong handshake, with a humorous welcoming compliment and, of course, that adorably impish smile!

No doubt within minutes the subject of recipes and cookbooks would have been front and foremost in our conversation. And why not? After all, James must have lived his cooking. How else could he have looked so comfortable in front of a television camera, a studio audience and millions of viewers, surrounded by raw, uncut ingredients, pots, pans, knives and spatulas and the prospect of producing yet another off-the-cuff, no-frills creation?

That's what I liked about the "Urban Peasant"—his down-to-earth simplicity, which is probably why his Ugly Vegetable and Sausage Stew (page 48) is one of my all-time favourite recipes and the one that never fails to remind me of James Barber—cook, entertainer and inspirer.

JILL GOWARD'S CHICKEN SANDWICH
2 SERVINGS

The quantities in this recipe are flexible and changing them won't spoil the taste. The combination of chicken, celery and walnuts appeals to everyone. Cheers, James!

½ stalk celery, finely chopped
1 cup [250 g] cold chopped cooked chicken
2 Tbsp [30 mL] finely chopped walnuts
Pinch of salt and pepper
Mayonnaise
Slices of lightly buttered bread

IN A BOWL, mix the celery, chicken and walnuts with salt and pepper and enough mayonnaise to moisten the mixture. Put a thick layer of it between the bread slices. Serve.

SORT-OF SOUVLAKI
2 SERVINGS

Sprig of oregano, chopped
¼ cup [50 mL] olive oil
Juice of 1 lemon
4 wooden skewers
1 whole boneless skinless chicken breast,
    cut into bite-sized pieces
Salt and pepper
1 tomato, chopped
½ English cucumber, chopped
½ cup [125 mL] yogurt
Pita bread

MIX THE OREGANO with the oil and lemon juice in a shallow dish. Soak the skewers in water for a few minutes, and then thread the chicken pieces onto the skewers. Season the chicken with a little salt and pepper and place the skewers in the dish containing the marinade. Marinate, refrigerated, for a couple of hours. If you are using a barbecue, let it heat up for 30 to 40 minutes before putting the skewers on it. Otherwise, heat a frying pan over medium-high heat for 5 minutes before putting the skewers in it. Cook the chicken for 6 to 8 minutes, brushing more of the marinade on it while it cooks, and turning once. Meanwhile, in a bowl combine the tomato, cucumber and yogurt. Serve the souvlaki with the yogurt mixture on the side and some fresh pita bread.

ORANGE AND LEMON CHICKEN
2 SERVINGS

For Valentine's Day—or any day.

2 boneless skinless chicken breasts
2 Tbsp [30 mL] all-purpose flour
2 Tbsp [30 mL] vegetable oil
2 stalks celery, chopped
1 Tbsp [15 mL] chopped fresh ginger
½ onion, chopped
1 cup [250 mL] white wine or apple juice

Zest and juice of 1 lemon
Zest and juice of 1 orange
Chopped mint
Salt and pepper

COAT THE CHICKEN breasts with flour. Heat the oil in a frying pan over high heat. Add the chicken and cook for 2 minutes on each side until nicely browned. Add the celery, ginger and onion, and cook a further 4 minutes, until the vegetables have softened. Stir in the wine, lemon and orange juices and zest, and some of the mint. Season with salt and pepper, reduce the heat to low, cover and simmer for 5 minutes. Garnish with the remaining mint and serve.

CHICKEN AND CASHEW CURRY
2 SERVINGS

3 Tbsp [45 mL] yogurt
1 tsp [5 mL] curry powder or to taste
1 whole boneless skinless chicken breast, cut
    into bite-sized pieces
1 Tbsp [15 mL] vegetable oil
1 Tbsp [15 mL] chopped fresh ginger
1 clove garlic, chopped
1 onion, chopped
Freshly ground pepper
Juice of ½ lemon
½ tsp [2 mL] dried chilies or to taste
2 Tbsp [30 mL] chopped green onions
2 Tbsp [30 mL] roasted cashews, chopped

COMBINE THE YOGURT and curry powder in a bowl and add the chicken pieces. Marinate (overnight if you wish). Heat the oil in a frying pan over medium-high heat, add the chicken pieces and cook until the outsides are well coloured. Stir in the ginger, garlic, onion, pepper, lemon juice and chilies, turn up the heat and cook for 5 to 10 minutes. Reduce the heat to medium, add the green onion and cashews, stir, and cook for 5 minutes. Serve.

Poultry & Meat

CHICKEN WITH RHUBARB

2 SERVINGS

The rhubarb gives a sweet-and-sour tanginess to this dish. It goes well with rice.

2 boneless skinless chicken breasts
2 Tbsp [30 mL] all-purpose flour
1 Tbsp [15 mL] curry powder
2 Tbsp [30 mL] vegetable oil
2 sticks rhubarb, finely chopped
1 onion, chopped
1 Tbsp [15 mL] brown sugar
1 tsp [5 mL] black pepper
1 tsp [5 mL] tarragon (or dill)
⅓ cup [75 mL] white wine
3 green onions, chopped
2 Tbsp [30 mL] chopped parsley

SHAKE THE CHICKEN, flour and curry powder together in a plastic bag. Remove the lightly dusted chicken. Heat the oil in a large, deep-sided frying pan over high heat and add the rhubarb and onion. Cook until softened and lightly browned, reduce the heat and stir in the brown sugar, pepper and tarragon. Push the mixture to the sides of the pan and place the chicken breasts in the middle. Brown the chicken for about 5 minutes each side, pour in the wine, and cook for 2 to 3 minutes to reduce the liquid. Add the green onion and parsley, stir well and serve immediately with rice.

MOROCCAN CHICKEN

2 SERVINGS

1 Tbsp [15 mL] lemon juice
1 tsp [5 mL] lemon zest
Handful of mint, chopped
Pinch of cayenne
Pinch of cinnamon
2 boneless skinless chicken breasts
10 dried apricots, chopped
2 oz [50 g] dried dates, chopped
¼ cup [50 mL] white wine
6-ounce [170 g] piece frozen puff pastry, thawed
1 egg
1 Tbsp [15 mL] milk
½ tsp [2 mL] superfine sugar

PREHEAT OVEN TO 400F [200C]. Combine the lemon juice and zest, mint, cayenne and cinnamon. Marinate the chicken in this mixture while preparing the other ingredients (or overnight if you can). In a small saucepan over low heat, cook the apricots and dates with the wine until most of the wine has been absorbed. Meanwhile, roll the pastry out to a ⅛-inch [3 mm] thickness, and cut out tops to fit two individual casserole dishes. Butter the casserole dishes, place one chicken breast in each and cover with the fruit. In a small bowl, combine the egg and milk. Place the pastry over top of the casserole dishes, and brush with the egg wash. Dust the top of the pastry with sugar and bake, uncovered, for 20 minutes, or until the pastry is nicely browned and the chicken is cooked through.

Dried apricots are great for hiking, snacks, lunch boxes and boat food, and as candy for kids. I used to get bad looks from kids at Halloween when I offered them a handful of dried fruit instead of bubblegum, but as the years went by, there appeared to be a hard core of kids who actually asked for fruit, which I thought was a triumph of common sense and proof of some nutritional instinct. Until I discovered that a local wheeler-dealer, aged ten, was trading in dried fruit, giving vast quantities of cheap candy for it, then selling it to his mother to make jam. —*Flash in the Pan*

CHICKEN BIRYANI

2 SERVINGS

Chicken and rice can be boring. This will make a chicken breast go a long way and cook in less than 30 minutes. Serve it with yogurt and chutney.

- 1 whole boneless skinless chicken breast, cut into ½-inch [1 cm] cubes
- Juice of ½ lemon
- ½ cup [125 mL] almonds (preferred) or peanuts
- 3 Tbsp [45 mL] vegetable oil
- 1 medium onion, halved and thinly sliced
- 2 cloves garlic, finely chopped
- 1 ¼-inch [3 cm] piece fresh ginger, slivered
- ½ tsp [2 mL] curry powder
- ½ tsp [2 mL] pepper
- ¼ tsp [1 mL] salt
- 1 cup [250 mL] uncooked basmati or long-grain rice
- 2 cups [500 mL] chicken stock or 1 chicken stock cube dissolved in 2 cups [500 mL] water

MARINATE CHICKEN in the lemon juice while you get everything else ready. Heat a large, dry frying pan over medium heat. Add the almonds and stir until they colour a bit (watch carefully so they don't burn). Remove the nuts from the pan and set aside. Add 1 Tbsp [15 mL] of the oil to the pan and cook the chicken over medium-high heat until brown. Set aside. Sauté the onion in the pan, stirring well, until light brown. Lower the heat, stir in the garlic and ginger, and cook for 2 minutes. Stir in the curry powder, pepper and salt, and cook for 30 seconds. Add the rice and stock, and turn the heat to medium-high. As soon as the mixture bubbles, turn the heat down as low as it will go, cover and cook for 10 minutes. Add the chicken and almonds to the rice, cover and cook for 5 minutes more. Serve.

CHICKEN JAMBALAYA

4 SERVINGS

New Orleans in a pot.

- 2 Tbsp [30 mL] vegetable oil
- 8 chicken thighs
- 1 clove garlic, chopped
- 1 sweet green pepper, chopped
- 1 onion, chopped
- 2 cups [500 mL] rice
- 4 whole cloves
- 1 bay leaf
- 1 Tbsp [15 mL] chili powder
- 1 tsp [5 mL] dried thyme
- ½ tsp [2 mL] cayenne
- 5 cups [1.25 L] stock or water
- Handful of parsley, chopped

HEAT THE OIL in a large pot or high-sided frying pan. Add the chicken and cook over high heat until browned on all sides. Remove the chicken from the pan and set aside. Add the garlic, green pepper and onion to the frying pan and cook over medium heat for 2 to 3 minutes. Add the rice, cloves, bay leaf, chili powder, thyme and cayenne, and cook for 3 minutes, until the rice is translucent. Stir in the stock and return the chicken to the pan. Bring to a boil, reduce the heat to low and simmer for about 30 minutes, until most of the liquid has been absorbed and the rice is done. Remove the bay leaf. Sprinkle the chicken with parsley and serve.

Poultry & Meat

PRINCESS PAMELA'S FRIED CHICKEN

6 SERVINGS

This recipe is named for Princess Pamela, who fed me dinner in New York City in the 1970s.

Lots of vegetable oil (not olive)
1 egg
½ cup [125 mL] milk
1 cup [250 mL] all-purpose flour
¼ cup [50 mL] cornmeal
1 tsp [5 mL] baking powder
½ tsp [2 mL] salt
Pinch of pepper
Pinch of paprika
6 pieces chicken (3 legs
   and 3 thighs are good)
1 can [14 oz/398 mL] peaches, drained
½ cup [125 mL] water
3 Tbsp [45 mL] brown sugar
1 Tbsp [15 mL] butter
1 Tbsp [15 mL] white vinegar
½ tsp [2 mL] paprika
Pinch of cayenne
Pinch of salt
Juice of 1 lemon

HEAT 1 INCH [2.5 CM] OIL in a high-sided saucepan over medium-high heat. As the oil heats, mix the egg and milk together in one bowl, and the flour, cornmeal, baking powder, salt, pepper and paprika in another bowl. Dip the chicken pieces into the milk mixture first, and then into the flour mixture. Fry the chicken pieces in the oil until golden brown, turning them as necessary. While the chicken cooks, combine the peaches, water, brown sugar, butter, vinegar, paprika, cayenne, salt and lemon juice in a saucepan and cook over medium heat until the mixture just starts to boil. Drain the chicken pieces on paper towels and let them cool for a minute. Then serve immediately with the sauce.

CHICKEN MOLE

4 SERVINGS

2 Tbsp [30 mL] vegetable oil
1 lb [500 g] tomatoes, chopped
2 onions, finely chopped
2 hot peppers, finely chopped
2 Tbsp [30 mL] finely chopped parsley
1 Tbsp [15 mL] finely chopped cilantro
½ tsp [2 mL] sugar
Freshly ground pepper
3 skinless chicken breasts, halved
2 pieces unsweetened chocolate, grated
1 tsp [5 mL] cumin
½ tsp [2 mL] cinnamon
Bay leaf
Handful of oregano, chopped
Juice of ½ lime
Chopped parsley or cilantro

HEAT THE OIL in a large frying pan over medium heat. Stir in the tomato, onion, hot peppers, parsley, cilantro and sugar, season with pepper and cook for abut 5 to 10 minutes. Add the chicken, chocolate, cumin, cinnamon, bay leaf, oregano and lime juice. Stir to combine and cook for 15 to 20 minutes. Remove the bay leaf. Serve the chicken garnished with chopped parsley.

for

VIJ'S YOGURT AND TAMARIND MARINATED GRILLED CHICKEN

SEE PAGE 153

UMBERTO MENGHI

CHEF, RESTAURATEUR, FOUNDER OF VILLA DELIA HOTEL AND TUSCANY COOKING SCHOOL, ITALY

*M*ost people discovered James through his show, his passion for food inspiring them to take a chance in the kitchen. James was a warrior and a lover—not afraid of showing his creativity through his recipes and always sticking a finger in the soup. He relished the practical challenges as well as the sensuality of cooking. To me, James Barber embodied "amichevole e divertente"—friendly and fun!

UMBERTO MENGHI'S INVOLTINI DI POLLO
(CHICKEN WITH RADICCHIO)
2 SERVINGS

2 chicken breasts
Salt and pepper
1 tsp [5 mL] finely chopped shallot or garlic
¼ tsp [1 mL] finely chopped oregano
1 cup [250 mL] chicken stock
4 Tbsp [60 mL] dry white wine or water
2 radicchio leaves
1 Tbsp [15 mL] all-purpose flour
¼ cup [50 mL] olive or vegetable oil
1 cup [250 mL] finely chopped tomato
2 slices [1 oz/25 g] mozzarella cheese
2 tsp [10 mL] finely chopped fresh parsley

PREHEAT OVEN TO 400F [200C]. Pound each chicken breast lightly to flatten it. Season with salt and pepper. Season one side of each breast with the chopped shallot and oregano.

In a saucepan, bring the chicken stock and 2 Tbsp [30 mL] of the wine to a boil over high heat. Add the radicchio and boil for 1 minute. Drain. Discard the cooking liquid.

Roll up each seasoned chicken breast in a radicchio leaf and secure with a wooden cocktail stick. Lightly dust the rolled chicken breasts with flour. Heat the oil in an ovenproof frying pan and sauté the chicken on both sides until lightly browned. Discard any excess oil from the pan and remove the cocktail sticks.

In a medium bowl, combine the remaining wine with the tomato and stir until well blended. Pour the tomato mixture over the chicken. Put a slice of mozzarella cheese on top of each piece. Bake for 12 to 15 minutes. Serve the chicken breasts on a warm serving platter or on warm plates and garnish with parsley.

Rock Cornish game hens are one of nature's drearier mistakes. Almost as though she had decided to make it all up to chickens for being so stupid and asked for a television studio to dream up a glamorous, pocket-sized image for them to aspire to. Rock Cornish game hens have no natural juices. What you usually end up with is a dried up-dwarf bird cowering in shame beneath a varnish of brown wallpaper paste. Small frozen birds (it sounds sad, but that's what these are) need moist cooking (like most ducks) and their juices need supplementing with onions and garlic and more fragrant spices.
—*Flash in the Pan*

TURKEY AND MINT TAGINE
4 SERVINGS

Serve this tagine with couscous salad and chopped mint.

2 Tbsp [30 mL] olive oil
10 whole cloves
6 whole cardamom pods
1 stick cinnamon
¾ lb [375 g] turkey meat, cubed
2 cups [500 mL] yogurt
1 cup [250 mL] chopped mint
2 Tbsp [30 mL] raisins
1 Tbsp [15 mL] coriander seeds
1 tsp [5 mL] cumin
1 tsp [5 mL] pepper
½ tsp [2 mL] salt
Cinnamon
Icing sugar

HEAT THE OIL with the cloves, cardamom and cinnamon over medium-high heat. Toss in the turkey cubes and brown them. Add the yogurt, mint, raisins, coriander seeds, cumin, pepper and salt; bring to a boil and cook until the mixture has thickened. Remove the cinnamon stick. Sprinkle the tagine with a little cinnamon and icing sugar. Serve.

CHRISTMAS CORNISH GAME HENS
2 SERVINGS

What comes out of this pot is a joy and delight, a particularly good Christmas dish—one bird apiece, fingers to lick, no oven to clean, no fuss, and a delicious aroma everywhere. Two-people Christmases are the ones you remember for a long time.

2 Tbsp [30 mL] olive oil
2 frozen Cornish game hens, defrosted
3 medium potatoes, quartered lengthwise
2 medium onions, peeled and left whole
1 clove garlic, chopped
1 can [19 oz/540 mL] diced tomatoes with
   red peppers
Large glass of red wine
Salt and pepper

HEAT THE OIL in a large pot over medium-high heat. Wipe the game hens dry and brown them in the oil for 5 minutes. Add the potato, onion and garlic, and toss to coat with oil. Add the tomato; stir and bring to a boil. Pour in the wine and season with salt and pepper, turn the birds in the sauce. Reduce the heat to low, cover and let cook for 1 hour, spooning the sauce over the birds every 15 minutes. If the sauce looks as if it's going to stick, add more wine. Light a candle, sing carols, drink the rest of the wine and enjoy the enticing aromas coming from the stove.

If there are leftovers, heat them up in a frying pan the next day with a chopped onion and a bit more red wine, and you have a quick Boxing Day pasta sauce.

Meat is meat. If the recipe calls for veal and you haven't got it or can't afford it, then use pork. Or chicken. Take a recipe like *piccata di vitello*, a very famous Italian dish. It calls for a slice of veal cut very thin, fried quickly in butter and then doused with lemon juice and a little white wine, some pepper and salt. I use chicken breasts instead of veal, beaten thin between lightly floured waxed paper, and sometimes I use pork, also beaten thin. Nobody knows the difference because people who come to dinner are not gourmets. They're just grateful. They get a free supper, and they haven't got to do the dishes. If the recipe calls for cider and you haven't got cider, then use apple juice. Or even beer. It will taste a bit different, but it will still taste nice. —*Cooking For Two*

DRUNKEN DUCK WITH GIN
2 SERVINGS

4 duck legs
1 carrot, grated
1 onion, chopped
5 to 6 whole cloves
1 Tbsp [15 mL] chopped orange zest
1 tsp [5 mL] dried rosemary
Bay leaf
Freshly ground pepper
¼ cup [50 mL] gin
Apple juice

PREHEAT OVEN TO 350F [180C]. Place the duck, carrot, onion, cloves, orange zest, rosemary, bay leaf and some pepper in a casserole dish, pour in the gin and apple juice, and bake, covered, for 1½ hours. Remove the bay leaf and serve.

Gin is not fashionable in kitchens. But if you learn to cook with it, you will always keep some on hand. It is food for rubbing backs, or cleaning false teeth, for thinning paint or anaesthetizing flies. In cooking, it does a lot for almost any drab meat.

Something happens in the cooking and, instead of a tame domesticated bland chicken or duck flavour, there comes a most aromatic smell and the taste of wild game, like partridges that have been feeding all summer on berries. —*Ginger Tea Makes Friends*

SPATCHCOCKED QUAIL AND GRAPES
4 SERVINGS

"Spatchcocked" means that the backbone of the quail (or other poultry) is cut out and the meat is flattened. Use a pair of kitchen scissors to do the job. You can do the same thing with Cornish game hens, but they will take twice as long to cook.

3 Tbsp [45 mL] olive oil
4 quails, spatchcocked
2 egg whites
4 Tbsp [60 mL] cornmeal
1 Tbsp [15 mL] butter
2 cloves garlic, chopped
½ cup [125 mL] almonds
½ cup [125 mL] seedless grapes
½ cup [125 mL] cilantro or parsley, chopped

HEAT THE OIL in a large frying pan over high heat. Dip the quails in the egg white and then the cornmeal. Place them in the frying pan and cook until brown on both sides, about 5 minutes for each side. Remove them from the frying pan and set them aside. Reduce the heat to medium-low and add the butter, garlic, almonds and grapes to the same frying pan. Cook for 2 to 3 minutes and then stir in the cilantro. Pour the sauce over the quails and serve immediately.

JERK ANYTHING
2 SERVINGS

Charmaine Crooks represented Canada in track and field at the Olympic Games five times. Her mother gave me this recipe. It's the key to everyone's heart in Jamaica.

6 chilies
4 cloves garlic
1 onion, coarsely chopped
1 cup [250 mL] water
¼ cup [50 mL] vinegar
4 Tbsp [60 mL] vegetable oil
1 Tbsp [15 mL] cumin
1 tsp [5 mL] sugar
Juice of 1 lime
Salt and pepper
2 boneless chicken breasts, pork chops or
    fillets of fish

PREHEAT OVEN TO 400F [200C]. In a food processor or blender, process the chilies, garlic, onion, water, vinegar, oil, cumin, sugar, lime juice, salt and pepper until the mixture is smooth. Place the meat or fish in an ovenproof dish. Pour the chili mixture over top and bake for 15 to 20 minutes for pork or chicken, 10 to 15 minutes for fish, or until done.

RACK OF LAMB
4 SERVINGS

Serve the lamb with some freshly baked bread for mopping up the juices.

2 (8 rib) racks of lamb
3 to 4 cloves garlic
1 can anchovies
1 Tbsp [15 mL] brown sugar
1 Tbsp [15 mL] soy sauce
Cherry tomatoes

PREHEAT OVEN TO 400F [200C]. Score the lamb in a diamond pattern. Place the garlic, anchovies, brown sugar and soy sauce in a blender and process to make a smooth paste. Rub the paste all over the lamb. Place the lamb on a rack over a pan and surround the lamb with some cherry tomatoes. Bake for 15 to 20 minutes. Serve the racks "cathedral-style"—upright with the bones interlocking—along with the cherry tomatoes.

LAMB WITH ORANGES
2 SERVINGS

This lamb dish goes well with rice or couscous.

2 Tbsp [30 mL] vegetable oil
1 clove garlic, chopped
1 small onion, chopped
6 lamb chops
1 orange, cut into eighths, skin left on
Sprig of mint, chopped

HEAT THE OIL in a large frying pan over high heat. Add the garlic and onion, and cook for 2 minutes. Push the onion mixture to one side of the pan and add the lamb chops. Cook for 2 minutes, turn the chops over, and cook for another 2 minutes. Squeeze the orange pieces over the lamb and add them and the mint to the pan. Cover and let cook for 5 minutes. Remove the orange pieces. Serve.

LAMB SKEWERS
WITH MINT AND YOGURT
2 SERVINGS

½ cup [125 mL] vegetable oil
2 Tbsp [30 mL] brown sugar
1 Tbsp [15 mL] tomato paste
½ lb [250 g] lamb shoulder, cubed
2 to 4 wooden skewers
½ cup [125 mL] plain yogurt
Sprig of mint, chopped

LIGHT YOUR BARBECUE, and while you wait for it to heat up, stir the oil, sugar and tomato paste together in a bowl. Add the cubed lamb and let it marinate in the oil mixture for 30 minutes. Soak the skewers in water for a few minutes. When your barbecue is good and hot, thread the lamb onto skewers and cook for 3 to 4 minutes. Turn the skewers over and cook for a further 3 minutes. Meanwhile, combine the yogurt and mint in a small bowl. Serve the yogurt dip alongside the lamb skewers.

QUICK LAMB CURRY WITH CHUTNEY
2 SERVINGS

Garnish this lamb curry with lime wedges and chopped cilantro and serve it with the chutney.

LAMB CURRY
2 Tbsp [30 mL] vegetable oil
1 onion, thinly sliced into rings
½ lb [250 g] lamb tenderloin, cut into bite-
   sized pieces
5 cloves garlic
1 apple, chopped
2 to 3 Tbsp [30–45 mL] sultanas
2 tsp [10 mL] curry powder
Juice of a lemon
1 cup [250 mL] water
2 Tbsp [30 mL] grated coconut

HEAT THE OIL in a large frying pan and sauté the onion rings over high heat. Add the lamb, garlic,

apple, sultanas, curry powder and lemon juice; stir well and cook until the lamb is until lightly browned. Pour in the water and add the grated coconut, reduce the heat and simmer for about 15 minutes, covered.

CHUTNEY
1 Tbsp [15 mL] chopped onion
1 Tbsp [15 mL] grated coconut
1 tsp [5 mL] sugar
Juice of ½ lemon
1 Tbsp [15 mL] grated carrot
1 Tbsp [15 mL] chopped parsley

PROCESS THE ONION, coconut, sugar and lemon juice in a blender, adding a little water if necessary. Stir in the carrot and parsley.

LAMB CHELO
4 SERVINGS

2 Tbsp [30 mL] vegetable oil
1 lb [500 g] stewing lamb, cut into bite-sized
   pieces.
8 to 10 dried apricots, chopped
1 clove garlic, chopped
1 large carrot, chopped
1 cup [250 mL] water
½ tsp [2 mL] cinnamon
½ tsp [2 mL] salt
⅛ tsp [0.5 mL] pepper
Handful of whole, blanched almonds

HEAT THE OIL in a stockpot over medium-high heat. Add the lamb and brown it quickly on all sides. Toss in the apricots, garlic and carrot, pour in the water and stir in the cinnamon, salt and pepper. Reduce the heat to low and simmer, covered, for 2 hours while you go on a bird-watching jaunt or to your weekly bridge game. Just before serving, toast the almonds in a dry frying pan over medium heat. Let the almonds cool a bit, chop them and serve the stew with the chopped almonds sprinkled over top.

Recollections of

SINCLAIR PHILIP

OWNER, SOOKE HARBOUR HOUSE, SOOKE, BC

64

Sinclair Philip

It was never dull being around James, whether for a cooking class, sharing a meal or just the enjoyment of watching him cook. I remember staying up late with James and Christina in their East Vancouver home in the '80s. We shared a wide range of delicious, simple dishes that he had prepared on the spur of the moment. I was regaled by stories of his work with the socialists in the French underground during World War II, slept on his couch and, only hours afterwards, got up early to go off to observe a cooking class he was conducting. James always got up very early in the morning, well before I wanted to. As we were leaving his house, I asked him where the cooking utensils were for the course. He always kept a complete, battered set in his car so that he was ready for any cooking adventure. He tossed the ingredients into the back of the car and, true to his race-car-driving past, off we roared into the streets of Vancouver to inspire yet another crowd of cooks anxious to learn from the master. James loved teaching and was very provocative with many of the aspiring cooks in his class. It was hands-on with no pretension. His students loved his classes and acquired a love of cooking and eating while they overcame their fear of cooking. He made cooking seem so simple. James always had a big female following, but it is amazing how many male university students and retirees took inspiration from his television shows and followed his recipes to the letter.

I continued to know James throughout the years afterward and dined out with him numerous times, invariably in Chinese or Thai restaurants. When we arrived at these restaurants, there was always an article he had written about them prominently displayed in their windows. Upon entering, you quickly understood what it was like to be treated like a king. At the Pink Pearl, dishes that weren't on the menu appeared without being ordered, and the best of Chinese wines, heated, were offered up to their dear friend James and his entourage. He might just as well have been the Emperor of China. He gave many of these restaurants the start and the recognition they needed, and these people will never forget him!

I last saw James at Bill Jones's annual summer party, where he entertained everyone with his stories about cooking sardines. He was in a great mood when he quipped, "Why don't British Columbians eat more of their sardines?" That day again, James chuckled away as he delighted in cooking local sardines, an expert and entertainer to the very end. James was famous from one end of Canada to the other and knew many movie stars and other celebrities, but he always believed in simple, real and delicious food that shouldn't be "mucked about" and that should be accessible to all. He will be missed. Think of James when you barbecue local sardines.

SOOKE HARBOUR HOUSE
FREE-RANGE RABBIT WITH MUSTARD SAUCE
4 TO 6 SERVINGS

Sinclair Philip

7 Tbsp [100 mL] Dijon-style mustard
1 free-range rabbit, skinned and cleaned,
    giblets removed (fryer or young rabbit)
2 Tbsp [30 mL] salted butter
2 Tbsp [30 mL] minced leek, white part only
2 Tbsp [30 mL] minced shallot
1 Tbsp [15 mL] minced garlic
⅓ cup [75 mL] dry Riesling wine
½ cup [125 mL] rabbit stock or chicken stock
½ cup [125 mL] whipping cream
Salt and pepper

PREHEAT OVEN TO 350F [180C]. Smear 6 Tbsp [90 mL] of the mustard over the rabbit and place it in a roasting pan. Roast the rabbit for 25 to 40 minutes, depending on the size of the rabbit. To test for doneness, make a small incision in the deepest part of the thigh and check that the meat has turned from light pink to white; if using a meat thermometer, the recommended internal temperature for rabbit is 160F [70C]. Be sure not to overcook or the rabbit will be very dry.

To prepare the sauce, melt the butter over low heat in a medium saucepan. Add the leek, shallot and garlic, and cook until translucent but not brown. Pour the Riesling into the pan, increase the heat to high and reduce the mixture until the pan is almost dry. Add the stock and continue to cook. When the liquid is reduced by half, stir in the whipping cream. Leave the pan on high heat and reduce again by half. Remove from the heat and whisk in the remaining mustard and season with salt and pepper.

Carve the rabbit and serve it with the sauce.

VENISON (BUT REALLY LAMB)

`4 SERVINGS`

Serve your favourite red cabbage dish with these chops.

1 cup [250 mL] cranberry juice
½ cup [125 mL] red wine
1 Tbsp [15 mL] vegetable oil
1 Tbsp [15 mL] chopped garlic
1 Tbsp [15 mL] chopped orange and lemon zest
1 Tbsp [15 mL] chopped parsley
1 Tbsp [15 mL] pepper
1 tsp [5 mL] cloves
1 tsp [5 mL] dried rosemary
8 lamb chops

IN A DISH, combine the cranberry juice, wine, oil, garlic, orange and lemon zest, parsley, pepper, cloves and rosemary. Marinate the lamb chops in this mixture for about 1 hour. Sauté the chops in a dry frying pan over high heat until done to your liking. Serve.

ISLAND PORK

`4 SERVINGS`

1 Tbsp [15 mL] vegetable oil
1 lb [500 g] pork tenderloin, sliced crosswise
2 cups [500 mL] chopped pineapple
1 ¼ tsp [6 mL] Dijon mustard
2 Tbsp [30 mL] rum
½ cup [125 mL] coconut milk
Salt and pepper
Chopped cilantro or parsley

HEAT THE OIL in a frying pan over high heat and brown the pork slices. Add the pineapple, Dijon mustard and rum; stir in the coconut milk and season with salt and pepper. Serve sprinkled with cilantro.

PATATAS VAREAS

`2 SERVINGS`

2 Tbsp [30 mL] olive oil
2 potatoes, cubed
2 anchovy fillets
3 cloves garlic
1 tsp [5 mL] tomato paste
1 spicy chorizo sausage, cubed
Chopped parsley

HEAT THE OIL in a frying pan and sauté the potatoes over high heat. When they're brown and crispy, add the anchovies, garlic and tomato paste. Stir well until the anchovies and tomato have blended in. Add the chorizo sausage. Stir once, turn the heat down and cook, covered, for 15 to 20 minutes. Serve with the parsley on top.

STEAMED GROUND PORK CHINESE-STYLE

`4 SERVINGS`

2 cups [500 mL] water
1 cup [250 mL] rice
½ 1b [250 g] ground pork
2 Tbsp [30 mL] sherry
2 Tbsp [30 mL] soy sauce
½ tsp [2 mL] five-spice powder or allspice
½ tsp [2 mL] pepper
Chopped cilantro

HEAT THE WATER and put the rice on to cook. Meanwhile, in a bowl combine the pork with the sherry, soy sauce, five-spice powder and pepper. Form the mixture into a large cake. Carefully place it on the cooking rice, cover and steam until the rice is done and has absorbed all the water. Remove the meat. Tip the rice onto a plate and garnish with cilantro. Place the meat cake on top and serve.

PORK, TERRIBLY SOPHISTICATED

4 SERVINGS

1 lb [500 g] pork tenderloin, sliced crosswise
2 Tbsp [30 mL] all-purpose flour
1 Tbsp [15 mL] vegetable oil
⅓ cup [75 mL] white wine
2 to 3 Tbsp [30–45 mL] cream
2 Tbsp [30 mL] cooked spinach
½ tsp [2 mL] grated nutmeg

PUT THE PORK in a plastic bag with the flour and flatten each piece of meat by beating it with a rolling pin or empty wine bottle. Heat the oil in a frying pan over high heat. Fry the pork pieces until brown on each side. Meanwhile, combine the wine, cream, spinach and nutmeg in a saucepan and blend into a purée. Pour this sauce onto a plate and top with the pork medallions.

PORK WITH APPLES

2 SERVINGS

A country dish from Normandy.

2 Tbsp [30 ml] vegetable oil
2 pork chops
2 cloves garlic, chopped
1 onion, chopped
1 apple, peeled and sliced
¼ cup [50 mL] apple juice
1 tsp [5 mL] dried thyme
2 Tbsp [30 mL] cream

HEAT THE OIL in a frying pan over high heat. Add the pork chops and cook, turning, until each side is nicely browned. Stir in the garlic and onion, and then add the apple. Cook for 2 minutes, and stir in the apple juice and thyme. Reduce the heat to medium, cover and cook for 10 minutes. Pour in the cream and heat it until scalding. Serve.

PORK STUFFED WITH PEAR AND GINGER

4 SERVINGS

1 lb [500 g] pork tenderloin
3 pears, chopped
2 green onions, chopped
½-inch [1 cm] piece fresh ginger, grated
2 Tbsp [30 mL] ricotta or cottage cheese
Salt and pepper
½ cup [125 mL] cider or apple juice

PREHEAT THE OVEN to 400F [200C]. Butterfly the tenderloin by cutting halfway through its width for its entire length. Open the butterflied tenderloin and place it between two sheets of waxed paper. Pound the pork with a rolling pin or empty wine bottle until it is flattened to a ¼-inch [5 mm] thickness. In a medium bowl, combine the pears, onion, ginger and ricotta, season with salt and pepper and spread the mixture down the centre of the pork. Roll up and tie the meat with string at intervals to keep it together. Place the rolled meat in a baking dish, pour the cider over top, cover and bake for 20 to 25 minutes. Let stand for 15 minutes. Slice and serve.

CABBAGE AND GARLIC SAUSAGE

2 SERVINGS

2 Tbsp [30 mL] vegetable oil
1 green cabbage, cut into 1-inch [2.5 cm] slices
1 onion, coarsely chopped
1 garlic sausage, cut into 1-inch [2.5 cm] slices
1 Tbsp [15 mL] pepper
1 tsp [5 mL] caraway seeds
½ tsp [2 mL] salt
½ cup [125 mL] water

HEAT THE OIL in a large frying pan and add the cabbage and onion. Turn the cabbage well to "bless" it with the hot oil. Toss in the garlic sausage, pepper, caraway seeds and salt, and pour in the water. Cook, covered, over medium heat for 10 to 15 minutes. Serve.

LENTILS WITH SAUSAGE (LENTEJAS CON MORCILLA)

`2 SERVINGS`

1 cup [250 mL] brown lentils, washed
2 ½ cups [625 mL] cold water
1 bay leaf
6 Tbsp olive oil
1 onion, finely chopped
½ cup [125 mL] chopped spicy sausage or
   bacon
3 cloves garlic, peeled
1 tsp [5 mL] all-purpose flour
½ tsp [2 mL] paprika
Salt and pepper

PUT THE LENTILS in a saucepan and cover with water. Add the bay leaf, bring to a boil, cover and simmer for 25 minutes. Drain, reserving some of the cooking liquid, and set aside. Heat the oil in a frying pan and sauté the onion and sausage until light brown. Add the garlic, flour and paprika. Stir well. Toss in the lentils, season with salt and pepper, and cook, stirring, for 2 to 3 minutes, adding extra lentil liquid if necessary. Remove the bay leaf. Serve.

HAM WITH CIDER SAUCE

`2 SERVINGS`

1 Tbsp [15 mL] butter
8 whole cloves
1 stick cinnamon or ½ tsp [2 mL] cinnamon
¼ cup [50 mL] brown sugar
¼ cup [50 mL] raisins
¼ tsp [1 mL] salt
1 cup [250 mL] cider
4 tsp [20 mL] cornstarch
2 thick ham steaks, cooked

TO MAKE THE SAUCE, melt the butter in a saucepan and stir in the cloves, cinnamon, brown sugar, raisins and salt. Pour in almost all the cider. Cook for 5 minutes. In a small bowl, mix the cornstarch with the remaining cider and add the mixture to the saucepan. Stir the sauce well until it thickens. Strain it and keep warm. Quickly fry the ham steaks to heat them through. Serve them with the sauce.

PIZZAIOLA

`4 SERVINGS`

4 quick-fry (thin-cut) pork chops
Milk
1 Tbsp [15 mL] olive oil
2 cloves garlic, chopped
2 onions, chopped
1 tsp [5 mL] tomato paste
1½ cups [375 mL] red wine
½ lb [250 g] cherry tomatoes
1 Tbsp [15 mL] capers
1 tsp [5 mL] dried oregano
Bay leaf
2 Tbsp [30 mL] chopped parsley

PLACE THE PORK chops in a dish and marinate them in milk for a few minutes. Meanwhile, heat the oil in a frying pan and stir in the garlic, onion and tomato paste. Add the wine, tomatoes, capers, oregano and bay leaf, and simmer, covered, until the tomatoes have blended into a sauce. Remove the pork chops from the milk. In another dry frying pan over high heat, quickly seal each side of the chops. Transfer the chops to the pan containing the sauce and cover them with it. Toss in the parsley and simmer for 5 minutes. Remove the bay leaf before serving the chops.

Recollections of

FRANÇOIS GAGNON

EXECUTIVE CHEF, CINCIN, VANCOUVER, BC

I arrived in Vancouver fresh out of the Centre intégré en alimentation et tourisme (CIAT) culinary program in Quebec, and with limited English. Watching *The Urban Peasant* was my first introduction to Anglophone television and inspired both my recipes and command of the English language.

CINCIN'S BBQ VEAL CHOPS WITH SALSA VERDE
4 SERVINGS

VEAL CHOP
4 veal chops, each 12-oz [350 g]
  (from Quebec preferably)
4 cloves garlic, squashed with the flat side of a knife
1 bunch thyme, chopped
1 tsp [5 mL] cracked peppercorns
Olive oil
Salt

APPROXIMATELY 8 TO 10 hours before dinner, rub the veal chops with garlic, thyme, cracked peppercorns and a few drops of olive oil. Place chops in an airtight container and refrigerate.

Remove seasoned chops from fridge and pre-heat barbecue to medium-low. Once the grill is hot, season the chops with salt and cook for 6 minutes on each side. Remove the chops from the grill, wrap in foil and allow to rest for 5 minutes. Garnish with Salsa Verde and serve.

continues on following page

continued from previous page

François Gagnon

SALSA VERDE
2 bunches Italian parsley
1 bunch chervil
¼ bunch cilantro
¼ bunch basil
¼ bunch mint
2 cups [500 mL] spinach leaves
1 tsp [5 mL] tarragon, chopped
1 tsp [5 mL] thyme, chopped
4 green onions, finely chopped
1 shallot, finely chopped
Zest of 1 lemon
2 Tbsp [30 mL] capers, chopped
About 1 cup [250 mL] extra virgin olive oil
Salt
Peppercorns
Lemon juice

RINSE ALL HERBS under water. Bring a pot of salted water to boil. Plunge the spinach in the boiling water for 5–10 seconds, then immediately transfer to an ice bath. Pat dry, removing all excess water from the spinach.

In a blender, add the leaves from the parsley, chervil, cilantro, basil and mint then add the spinach and blend, slowly adding enough olive oil to allow the purée to run smoothly through the blender.

In a bowl, mix purée, tarragon, thyme, green onion, shallot, zest and capers with a spatula. Season with salt, pepper and lemon juice to taste. Leftover Salsa Verde can be refrigerated for 5–6 days in an airtight container.

Stir-frying is the first basic technique of Chinese cooking. You don't need a wok or any special equipment, just a good big frying pan and a tool to turn things over. Successful stir-frying needs only three things: complete concentration for 5 minutes, a hot pan and everything else ready—the table set, the wine chilled, the butler ready, the maids in clean aprons and the Châteauneuf-du-pape decanted. You get ready, you get set and you go. Just make sure that everything's fresh—looking for fresh green beans without black spots on them is a pleasant way to spend a Saturday morning—because in Chinese cooking, texture is as important as flavour. —*Mushrooms Are Marvellous*

GREEN BEAN STIR-FRY WITH PORK

2 SERVINGS

This recipe can also be made with ground beef and runner beans.

1 Tbsp [15 mL] vegetable oil
½ lb [250 g] ground pork
1 clove garlic, finely chopped
1 onion, coarsely chopped
Ginger
½ tsp [2 mL] cornstarch
1 Tbsp [15 mL] vinegar
1 Tbsp [15 mL] soy sauce
1 tsp [5 mL] sugar
1 tsp [5 mL] sesame oil
Hot red pepper
Salt and pepper
½ lb [250 g] long Chinese beans, cut Into finger-length pieces

HEAT THE OIL in a frying pan over high heat and brown the pork. Add the garlic, onion and ginger, stir well and cook for 2 to 3 minutes. In a small bowl, mix the cornstarch with the vinegar. Add the cornstarch mixture to the pork, along with the soy sauce, sugar, sesame oil, hot red pepper, salt and pepper. Toss in the beans, coat them with the sauce and cook until the beans are tender. Serve immediately.

PORTUGUESE PORK AND CLAMS

4 SERVINGS

3 Tbsp [45 mL] vegetable oil
1 lb [500 g] pork tenderloin, cut into bite-sized pieces
2 cloves garlic, chopped
2 tomatoes, chopped
1 stalk celery, chopped
1 sweet green pepper, chopped
1 small onion, chopped
½ cup [125 mL] white wine
1 bay leaf
Pinch of paprika
1 lb [500 g] small fresh clams, in the shell
2 sprigs of cilantro, chopped

HEAT THE OIL in a saucepan over medium-high heat. Add the pork and cook until browned on all sides, about 6 minutes. Remove the pork from the saucepan and set aside. In the same saucepan, cook the garlic, tomato, celery, green pepper and onion for 2 to 3 minutes. Add the wine, bay leaf and paprika, and cook for a further 10 minutes. Toss in the clams and cook, covered, until the clams have opened, about 8 minutes. Discard any clams that do not open. Return the pork to the saucepan, and cook for another 2 minutes. Remove the bay leaf before serving. Top with cilantro.

BILL JONES

CHEF, COOKBOOK AUTHOR, FOOD CONSULTANT AND EDUCATOR, DEERHOLME FARM, DUNCAN, BC

When I first met James, I had a good clue who he was. At the time his face was plastered on TV screens and book covers. I can honestly say (looking back at that first meeting) that I had no clue what he was. He was above all a very intriguing man, always willing to surprise and sometimes shock the unsuspecting world around him. Our relationship started as professional and mutual regard and ended up as an overlapping of our respective families. We both lived in the Cowichan Valley and worked together on many events, fundraisers, cooking classes and projects. Getting to know James was like peeling off the layers of an onion—oh, you were an engineer, really? You speak fluent French and German, really? You had tea with the emperor of Japan, really? Aside from the facts of each layer there was always a good story attached to it. "Yeah, I had tea with the emperor—along with a thousand other people. I thought it was a personal invitation. Bit of a blow to the ego, really."

It has always amused me greatly that this textured and complex man preached a message of simplicity. "Slow down," he used to say. "Don't stress over something as simple as food. Share the experience with your loved ones and don't be afraid to make a mess in the process." This apparently was a message that people loved to hear. The public would flock to his side during an event or cooking demo. "We watch your show all the time," they'd say. "I watched you, too," he replied. "I always wave and you never waved back."

James became a mentor and close friend to me. His generosity of spirit, zest for life and sharp intellect taught me many valuable lessons. Some people remember him as a figure larger than life. I remember him as a man who was a willing partner of life. He was an active participant in the world around him, always ready for new experiences and challenges. He grabbed each day like it was a fresh start on life. That was truly something to marvel at and was inspirational to me and a lot of other folk.

This is my favourite James Barber recipe:

TOMATO, BREAD AND BASIL SOUP

I don't know if this recipe exists in a book or just flowed out of James's mind. He loved to make this dish in public.

TAKE A POT with a lid and add 6 whole tomatoes, a chopped onion, 2 cups [500 mL] of liquid (water, wine, cider) and as much chopped garlic as you can stand. Cover with the lid and cook for about 5 minutes, or until the tomato starts to break down. Mash the tomato with a spoon to break up the big chunks. Take a loaf of French bread and break off about 2 cups [500 mL] worth of small chunks, add them to the soup along with 2 tablespoons [30 mL] of chopped basil. Cook for another couple of minutes. Stir well to blend the bread and juices and season with salt and pepper. Serve hot.

People always loved this simple and comforting soup—made with a minimum of ingredients and a minimum of chopping. To me, it is pure genius.

BILL JONES'S GRILLED FLATIRON STEAK WITH TUSCAN BREAD SALAD

James loved to barbecue. We made this recipe, which turns a relatively inexpensive cut of meat into a work of art, as part of a grilling class at my farm. This cut of beef is best cooked to medium-rare and left to stand for 10 minutes before carving, to distribute the juices in the meat. The salad is another variation on the tomato and bread theme and is an exercise in simplicity, freshness and great taste. Use ripe tomatoes and a good rustic bread for the best results. Truly a meal fit for an Urban Peasant.

STEAK
2 lb [1 kg] flatiron steak (or flank steak)
1 cup [250 mL] beer
1 Tbsp [15 mL] chopped garlic
1 Tbsp [15 mL] chopped mixed herbs (sage, rosemary, oregano)
Salt and pepper

SALAD
4 cups [1 L] rustic bread,
    cut into 1-inch [2.5 cm] chunks
2 tomatoes, cut into chunks
½ cup [125 mL] olives (mixed, green, kalamata, etc.)
2 Tbsp [30 mL] extra virgin olive oil
1 Tbsp [15 mL] balsamic vinegar
1 Tbsp [15 mL] red wine vinegar
2 Tbsp [30 mL] chopped fresh basil
Salt and pepper

PLACE THE STEAK, beer, garlic and mixed herbs in a glass casserole. Season with salt and pepper and let stand for at least 1 hour.

Grill the steak on a hot grill to the desired degree of cooking—about 5 minutes per side. Remove the steak from the heat, cover with aluminum foil and let stand for 10 minutes.

Meanwhile, in a large bowl combine the bread cubes, tomato, olives, olive oil, balsamic and red wine vinegars and basil. Season well with salt and pepper, and toss the mixture to distribute the oil and vinegar.

Slice the steak very thinly. Place a little bread salad on each plate and top with slices of steak. Enjoy!

BARBECUED FLANK STEAK

If you like steak, try this. A flank steak has no waste and no bones, it's enough for dinner and there will be leftovers for beef salad the next day.

1½ lb [750 g] flank steak
Salt and pepper
No oil no oil no oil

HEAT THE BARBECUE for 15 minutes to get it really hot. Sprinkle the steak with salt and pepper, throw it on the centre of the barbecue, close the lid and grill the steak for 4 minutes exactly. Flip it over, close the lid again quickly and cook the steak for 3 minutes exactly. (Cooking it any longer will make it tough.) Remove the steak from the grill and let stand for 5 minutes. Slice it very thinly across the grain and serve immediately.

BEEF WITH ORANGES

2 SERVINGS

½ lb [250 g] flank steak or skirt steak
2 Tbsp [30 mL] vegetable oil
1 Tbsp [15 mL] soy sauce
1 tsp [5 mL] cornstarch
Pepper
1 orange
2 cloves garlic, chopped
1-inch [2 cm] piece fresh ginger, grated
1 tsp [5 mL] dried chili pepper
1 cup [250 mL] cherry tomatoes

SLICE THE STEAK thinly, across the grain, and place the slices in a bowl. In another bowl, combine 1 Tbsp [15 mL] of the oil with the soy sauce, cornstarch and some pepper. Pour the mixture over the beef. Zest the orange or cut thin strips of the peel off and chop them up. Heat the remaining oil in a frying pan over medium-high heat. Add the garlic and ginger to the frying pan and stir. Add the beef and its marinade, along with the orange zest, chili pepper and tomatoes.

Cut the orange in half and squeeze the juice into the pan. Stir and cook for 6 minutes or so, or until the beef is cooked and a nice sauce has formed in the pan. Serve.

BEEF BROCHETTES

2 SERVINGS

These brochettes are great with mashed potatoes.

2 to 4 wooden skewers
½ lb [250 g] beef tenderloin,
    cut into bite-sized pieces
2 Tbsp [30 mL] vegetable oil
2 Tbsp [30 mL] Dijon mustard
2 tomatoes, chopped
1 small onion, chopped
Sprig of rosemary, chopped
Salt and pepper
¼ cup [50 mL] water

SOAK THE SKEWERS in water for a few minutes. Thread the beef pieces onto the skewers. Heat the oil in a frying pan over medium-high heat. Brush a thin layer of mustard on the beef, place the skewers in the frying pan and brown each side. Add the tomato and onion, and cook for 2 to 3 minutes. Stir the vegetables and turn the skewers over. Sprinkle with rosemary and a little salt and pepper, and cook the beef for another 2 minutes. Remove the beef from the pan and set aside. Add the water to the pan and bring the tomato mixture to a boil. Pour the sauce over the beef and serve.

ĆEVAPČIĆI

2 SERVINGS

1 egg
½ lb [250 g] ground beef
3 to 4 Tbsp [45–60 mL] finely chopped onion
1 Tbsp [15 mL] chopped parsley
1 tsp [5 mL] dried oregano
1 tsp [5 mL] paprika
Freshly ground pepper

2 Tbsp [30 mL] vegetable oil
1 tomato, chopped
⅓ bottle beer
½ tsp [2 mL] salt

IN A BOWL, stir the egg, ground beef, onion, parsley, oregano, paprika and pepper together well. Heat the oil in a frying pan over medium-high heat. Form the beef mixture into finger-length sausages and place them in the frying pan. Turn them when browned and reduce the heat. Push the beef to one side, add the tomato, beer and salt, and cook for a few minutes more. Serve.

KORMA
2 SERVINGS

Very bright, very colourful, and of course, very easy. Most of the cooking happens while you're doing something else, so that life doesn't have to come to a grinding halt just because you've got people coming to supper. Korma is a curry but it's not intended to be a biker's special or an alternative to Drano. It will not make your hair fall out or smoke come out of your ears. It's mild and gentle and rich. And foolproof.

You can also use pork tenderloin to make this korma. Serve it with rice, chapattis or chickpeas.

2 cloves garlic, chopped
½ lb [250 g] beef tenderloin,
    cut into bite-sized pieces
½ cup [125 mL] full-fat plain yogurt
½ tsp [2 mL] turmeric
2 Tbsp [30 mL] vegetable oil
1 small onion, chopped
2 whole cloves
½ tsp [2 mL] cinnamon
½ tsp [2 mL] pepper
Pinch of salt
¼ cup [50 mL] water

MIX THE GARLIC, meat, yogurt and turmeric together in a bowl and let stand, refrigerated, for between 2 and 6 hours. When ready to cook, heat

the oil in a frying pan over medium-high heat. Add the onion, cloves, cinnamon, pepper and salt to the pan, and cook for 2 to 3 minutes. Add the meat with the yogurt mixture and the water; stir everything together and cover and simmer for 45 minutes. Check on it once in a while, making sure it doesn't get too dry (if it does, just add more water). Discard the cloves before serving the korma. Serve.

MUSHROOM BEEF BURGERS
4 SERVINGS

Fried or barbecued, these hamburgers have a lovely rich texture and are moist and comforting. I serve them on thick slices of toasted French bread, and sometimes, to make them a bit more fancy, I spread a little snail butter (Poor Man's Escargots, page 18) on them.

¼ lb [125 g] mushrooms, coarsely chopped
2 Tbsp [30 mL] butter
1 egg
1 clove garlic, chopped
1 medium onion, chopped
1 lb [500 g] ground beef
2 Tbsp [30 mL] parsley, chopped
1 tsp [5 mL] dried thyme or oregano
1 tsp [5 mL] salt
½ tsp [2 mL] aniseed
½ tsp [2 mL] nutmeg
½ tsp [2 mL] pepper
All-purpose flour
2 Tbsp [30 mL] vegetable oil

IN A FRYING PAN over medium heat, fry the mushrooms in the butter for 2 minutes. Put them in a bowl with the egg, garlic, onion, beef, parsley, thyme, salt, aniseed, nutmeg and pepper. Squish the ingredients together with your hands until well mixed. Shape the mixture into patties as thick as your big toe; pat them well so that they stay together. If frying, sprinkle both sides of the patties with flour, heat the oil and fry them for a maximum of 4 minutes on each side. If barbecuing, first brush the patties with oil (omit the flour).

Recollections of

PINO POSTERARO

COOKBOOK AUTHOR AND EXECUTIVE CHEF AND OWNER,
CIOPPINO'S MEDITERRANEAN GRILL AND ENOTECA, VANCOUVER, BC

To me, James had the essence of a real person. Therefore his food, like him, was real. His superficial exterior was rustic, but deep down he had a noble and sensitive soul.

PINO POSTERARO'S BARBECUED RIB-EYE OF PRIME BEEF ALLA FIORENTINA
4 SERVINGS

Instead of serving the traditional beef alla Fiorentina, or porterhouse steak, I use rib-eye, which is more service- and customer-friendly because it is a smaller cut. Just like the classic, the meat is marinated and served rare.

4 beef rib-eye steaks (each 5 oz/150 g), fat trimmed
   and silver skin removed
4 Tbsp [60 mL] olive oil
2 Tbsp [30 mL] balsamic vinegar
1 tsp [5 mL] sherry vinegar
4 Tbsp [60 mL] chopped mixed herbs (rosemary, sage, thyme)
1 clove garlic, chopped
Black pepper
Salt
2 cups [500 mL] baby arugula
16 cherry tomatoes
1 small minced shallot
4 Tbsp [60 mL] Basic Vinaigrette (page 119)
Shaved Parmesan cheese

PLACE THE STEAKS in a glass or stainless steel dish. Drizzle them with the olive oil and balsamic and sherry vinegars, and sprinkle each side of the steaks with the mixed herbs, garlic and black pepper. Allow the steaks to marinate at room temperature for 45 minutes to 1 hour.

Preheat barbecue to high. Remove the steaks from the marinade, discard it, and season them with salt. Cook the steaks for 8 minutes per side for rare (10 to 12 minutes per side for medium-rare). Remove the steaks from the grill and let stand.

In a medium bowl, toss the arugula and cherry tomatoes with the shallot and vinaigrette.

To serve, slice the steaks and top each with the arugula salad. Finish with a sprinkling of shaved Parmesan.

SEAFOOD

SQUID THAI-STYLE
4 SERVINGS

12 squid, cleaned
1 Tbsp [15 mL] vegetable oil
½ lb [250 g] ground pork
7 to 8 hot peppers, whole
2 to 3 cloves garlic, chopped
2 slices fresh ginger, chopped
1 bunch mint, chopped
Juice of 1 lime
Cilantro

CUT OPEN THE SQUID tubes, lay them flat and, using a sharp knife, score them in a diamond pattern. Then cut the squid into bite-sized pieces and set aside. Heat the oil in a frying pan. Add the pork and peppers and, stirring vigorously, cook over a high heat for 5 minutes. Stir in the garlic and ginger, and continue cooking until the pork is cooked. Combine the squid with the pork mixture, and then stir in the mint and lime juice. Cook for 2 minutes. Serve on a plate garnished with cilantro.

SCALLOP AND POTATO FLAN
2 SERVINGS

4 new potatoes, boiled, peeled and thinly
    sliced
Salt and pepper
¼ lb [125 g] scallops, sliced into thin rounds
Dollop of butter
1 lemon, cut into 6 slices
¼ tomato, cut into small cubes
Sprig of parsley, chopped

PREHEAT OVEN TO 375F [190C]. Butter two 1-cup [250 mL] ramekins. Arrange a layer of potato on the bottom of each ramekin. Season lightly with salt and pepper. Arrange a layer of scallops over the potato, and the remaining potato on top of the scallops. Season again with salt and pepper, and drop a dollop of butter on top. Layer the lemon slices on top of the

butter. Bake, uncovered, for 15 minutes or until the flans are bubbling. When they have finished baking, flip them upside down onto a plate and garnish with tomato and parsley.

SCALLOPS WITH MUSHROOMS
2 SERVINGS

3 cloves garlic, chopped
2 Tbsp [30 mL] butter
2 Tbsp [30 mL] olive oil
4 green onions, chopped
¼ lb [125 g] small mushrooms, very fresh
    and innocent-looking
½ lb [250 g] fresh scallops
3 Tbsp [45 mL] dried bread crumbs
4 Tbsp [60 mL] chopped parsley
½ tsp [2 mL] salt
¼ tsp [1 mL] pepper

IN A FRYING PAN over low heat, fry the garlic in 1 Tbsp [15 mL] of the butter and 1 Tbsp [15 mL] of the oil for 1 minute (no longer or the garlic will brown and become bitter). Add the green onion and mushrooms, and cook for 2 minutes. Increase the heat to medium-high, add the scallops and cook for 2 to 4 minutes (depending on their size). Meanwhile, in another frying pan, mix the remaining butter and oil, and fry the bread crumbs until crisp. Drain any liquid from the scallops. Stir the fried bread crumbs, parsley, salt and pepper into the scallop mixture. Serve immediately.

SHRIMP EGG FOO YONG

4 SERVINGS

You can substitute canned shrimp for the fresh shrimp in this recipe.

4 tsp [20 mL] vegetable oil
1 carrot, finely chopped
1 clove garlic, finely chopped
1 onion, finely chopped
1 stalk celery, finely chopped
½ lb [250 g] fresh shrimp, peeled, deveined and rinsed
6 eggs
½ tsp [2 mL] salt
Freshly ground pepper
2 handfuls bean sprouts
Chopped cilantro

HEAT 2 TSP [10 ML] of the oil over medium heat in a frying pan. Sauté the carrot, garlic, onion and celery until tender. Add the shrimp and cook until they just turn pink. Remove the mixture from the frying pan and set aside. Break the eggs into a bowl and mix in the salt and pepper. Toss in the bean sprouts and combine. Heat the remaining oil in the frying pan and pour in the egg and sprouts mixture. Cook for 2 minutes until set. Slide the egg mixture halfway onto a plate, top with the shrimp mixture and fold over the other half. Garnish with cilantro.

SPANISH PRAWNS, GARLIC AND CHILIES (GAMBAS AL AJILLO)

2 SERVINGS

In Spain, these prawns are brought to the table covered with sliced bread to stop the oil from spitting and with which to mop up the flavourful juices.

½ cup [125 mL] olive oil
2 red chilies, chopped
5 cloves garlic, chopped
1 lb [500 g] prawns, peeled
¼ cup [50 mL] chopped parsley
Salt

1 baguette, thickly sliced
1 lemon, cut into wedges

HEAT THE OIL in a wok or a high-sided saucepan over medium-high heat. Add the chilies and cook for 1 to 2 minutes. Toss in the garlic and prawns, and, stirring constantly, cook for 2 to 3 minutes, or until the prawns just turn pink. Stir in the parsley and season with salt. Place the prawn mixture on two plates, top with a slice of bread and serve immediately with lemon wedges and extra bread.

CARIBBEAN SHRIMP

4 SERVINGS

1 onion, chopped
2 Tbsp [30 mL] butter
1 sweet red pepper, chopped
1 cup [250 mL] cooked rice
½ tsp [2 mL] chili powder
½ tsp [2 mL] salt
Chopped garlic (optional)
½ lb [250 g] fresh shrimp, peeled, deveined and rinsed
2 bananas
½ cup [125 mL] cream
Lettuce leaves, washed and dried
Twists of lemon peel

IN A FRYING PAN over a medium heat, sauté the onion in the butter. Stir in the red pepper and cooked rice, mixing well. Add in the chilli powder, salt and garlic (if using), and then the shrimp. Peel and slice the bananas, add them to the shrimp mixture, pour in the cream and combine. Cook for a few minutes, until the bananas and cream are heated through. Serve the shrimp mixture on lettuce leaves garnished with lemon twists.

When it comes to cooking fish there is a simple rule, invented some thirty years ago by the Department of Fisheries and quoted by cookbooks all over the world, that is known as "The Canadian Rule."

It's easy. You lay the fish on its side (steaks, fillets, whole fish, just lay them all flat), measure the thickness at the thickest part of the fish, and cook it 10 minutes per inch [2.5 cm] of thickness. Frying pan, hot oven, steamer or barbecue—salmon, cod, snapper or skate—whatever you choose, 10 minutes an inch. I personally think that's a *little* too much, and I suggest 8 minutes, but start with 10 and you won't go wrong. (10 minutes an inch is the absolute maximum!)

Flour sticks to fish and makes a crispy skin on the outside, which seals in the juices and keeps it moist. Cornmeal won't stick unless you first dip the fish in milk, but cornmeal will give it a crunchy texture that is very pleasant with white fishes like cod fillets or snapper. If you want extra flavour, mix pepper, salt and a little thyme (very French) into the flour, or a little sugar and red cayenne pepper, which will give it a hot and sweet crispiness (very Northern Chinese). —*Peasant's Alphabet*

GREEK-STYLE PRAWNS WITH FETA
2 SERVINGS

These prawns are perfect with rice.

¼ cup [50 mL] olive oil
2 green onions, chopped
1 clove garlic, chopped
1 sweet red pepper, chopped
Handful of parsley, chopped
Sprig of oregano, chopped
2 tomatoes, chopped
½ cup [125 mL] white wine
Splash of milk
12 prawns, peeled, deveined and rinsed
Salt and pepper
¼ cup [50 mL] crumbled feta cheese

HEAT THE OIL in a saucepan over medium heat. Add the green onion, garlic, red pepper, parsley and oregano, and cook for 5 minutes, until the onion has softened. Add the tomato, wine and milk, and cook for 20 minutes. Toss in the prawns and cook until they just turn pink, about 2 minutes. Season with salt and pepper. Sprinkle the crumbled feta on top and serve with rice.

PAPAYA BUTTER FOR GRILLED FISH
MAKES ABOUT 1 CUP [250 ML]

1 ripe papaya, peeled and coarsely chopped
½ cup [125 mL] unsalted butter
3 Tbsp [45 mL] white wine
2 tsp [10 mL] lime juice
2 tsp orange juice

BLEND THE PAPAYA, butter, wine, lime juice and orange juice in a food processor. Chill. Serve with grilled fish.

SHIOYAKE

SPRINKLE A LITTLE salt on a plate. Place some salmon or other fish fillets skin-side down on the salt and let stand for at least 10 minutes. Put the fillets into a hot, dry pan with the skin side down and cook for about 5 to 10 minutes with the lid on. Serve garnished with lemon slices.

My first real boat was an ancient amateur re-rigged 2½-ton Hilyard, a gaff-rigged sloop, without winches and before nylon, which meant that trimming sail or even just going about was a complicated, back-straining, palm-stripping process. It involved a sophisticated method of jiggling wooden blocks and an even more sophisticated method of steering, known as "bumlock." You can figure that one out for yourself—single-handed, helm hard over because she went across the wind slower than a haltered cow, and since I needed both hands to trim and cleat the mainsheet, the only way to steer and get back up into the wind was to grab the tiller with the seat of my pants. In those days the Solent (on the south coast of England) was a good place to fish for mackerel, which, like tuna, are attracted to just about anything bright and shiny that flutters in the water like a wounded fish. I learned this the hard way. A hand-held rod will always catch more fish than one in a mounted rod holder because there's more movement to it. Anybody holding a rod naturally wriggles about, grabs a beer, reads the chart and takes a deep breath, and all these small movements are transmitted to the lure in the water. I always dragged a line over the stern and twitched it occasionally without much luck, but I could be just about a hundred percent sure of hooking a fish at the moment of most activity, right at the crucial moment of going about, both hands (and buttocks) busy, the boat dickering in stays and the little bell on the line saying fish fish fish. And by the time we were about, settled down on the new tack, a bigger fish had eaten the back half of my mackerel and left me with the head. The same thing happened to me a couple of years ago off Cape Mudge, where the rockfish we caught close to the kelp beds were grabbed by opportunistic lingcod. The moral of this story is if you've got fish, do something about it immediately. That is also the best counsel anybody can give you when it comes to cooking fish. The quicker you can get it into the pan, the better it's going to taste, and the less you do to it, the better. We used to haul in the mackerel, gut it, crank up the Primus right there in the cockpit, and cook it in a dry fry pan liberally dusted with coarse salt. —*One-Pot Wonders*

SALMON WITH GINGER
1 SERVING

1 salmon steak
2 slices fresh ginger, chopped
½ tsp [2 mL] hot red pepper
1 tsp [5 mL] butter

FOLD THE EDGES of some foil to form a tray big enough to hold the salmon steak. Place it on the foil and sprinkle the ginger and hot red pepper over it. Dot with butter and place in the toaster oven on high, or broil for about 5 minutes.

MISO SALMON
2 SERVINGS

Of the endless ways to serve salmon, this is one of my favourites—it's not too heavy and has lots of complex flavours.

4 Tbsp [60 mL] miso paste*
2 Tbsp [30 mL] white wine or apple juice
1 Tbsp [15 mL] honey
1 clove garlic, chopped
1 tsp [5 mL] sugar
½ tsp [2 mL] powdered ginger
2 salmon steaks

IN A SMALL BOWL, combine the miso paste, wine, honey, garlic, sugar and ginger. Brush the miso mixture onto the salmon steaks. Heat a dry frying pan over high heat and fry the steaks for 8 minutes per finger thickness of fish, turning once. Serve.

*Available at Japanese markets.

Canned fish shouldn't be the last resort of the desperate. Sardines make great sandwiches with a little mayonnaise and some thinly sliced green onions, sockeye salmon makes wonderful fish cakes (and even a quick stir-fry), canned tuna takes on a whole new dimension with a couple of hard-boiled eggs and some black olives, and canned clams work well in chowder with a little extra garlic.

Astronauts don't carry can openers, but any two earthbound people setting up house should make sure they have a little stock of canned fish. —*Cooking For Two*

PAN-ROASTED SALMON
WITH SWEET PEPPERS AND GARLIC
2 SERVINGS

1 Tbsp [15 mL] olive oil
3 cloves garlic, thinly sliced
2 sweet red or yellow peppers, chopped
2 salmon steaks
⅓ cup [75 mL] white wine or apple juice
½ tsp [2 mL] dried thyme
Pinch of cayenne
Salt and pepper
Chopped parsley

HEAT THE OIL in a frying pan over high heat and add the garlic and peppers. Cook for 2 minutes, stirring constantly. Push the peppers to one side of the pan and lay the salmon steaks beside them. Cook for 1 minute, turn the fish and pour in the wine. Sprinkle the fish with thyme and cayenne, season with salt and pepper and spoon the peppers over the fish. Cover, reduce the heat and cook for 6 minutes. Sprinkle with parsley and serve.

SPINACH PANCAKES
WITH CANNED SALMON
4 SERVINGS

2 Tbsp [30 mL] butter
4 Tbsp [60 mL] all-purpose flour
1¼ cups milk
3 eggs
1 pkg [300 g] frozen spinach, thawed, squeezed dry and chopped
½ cup [125 mL] shredded cheddar cheese
About 1 Tbsp [15 mL] melted butter
1 can [7.5 oz/213 g] salmon, drained and flaked
2 Tbsp [30 mL] mayonnaise
1 tsp [5 mL] curry powder

MELT THE BUTTER in a saucepan over medium heat. Stir in the flour and cook, stirring vigorously, for 1 minute. Slowly add the milk and cook until the sauce thickens, about 3 minutes. Remove from the heat, cool slightly and beat in the eggs, spinach and cheese. Heat a frying pan over medium heat, brush with a little melted butter and pour in a thin layer of batter, tilting the pan so the batter spreads evenly. Cook until the top is just dry. Remove the pancake to a plate and cook another. Mix the salmon, mayonnaise and curry powder together in a small bowl. Spread this filling between the cooked pancakes, stacking them on top of one another. Slice the stack carefully into wedges and serve.

Recollections of

HIDEKAZU TOJO

EXECUTIVE CHEF AND OWNER, TOJO'S RESTAURANT, VANCOUVER, BC

I first met James in 1972, a year after my arrival to Vancouver, in a Japanese restaurant called Maneki, where I was working. He would come occasionally for lunch, sit at the sushi bar and try all sorts of Japanese dishes.

The way I see it, James was a real, true food writer. I say this because of his pure passion for food. I believe it was a sheer joy for him to taste all types of food from any culinary tradition. He would approach food, any food, without any preconceptions, taste it, and then write honest comments. Other food critics were generally hesitant to try things that were too alien from the food culture they were accustomed to. For example, when they covered Japanese food, they would eat raw *maguro* (tuna) at the most and refrain from eating more "exotic" things such as squid and octopus—although they would not refrain from writing about them as though they knew all about them. James, on the other hand, was happy to try the most interesting dish that I had to offer. He did not let others tell him what to eat, what to avoid, what was good or

what was repulsive. He was not deterred by presumptions. He showed that a true food lover saw no cultural boundaries. To me, he epitomized how a true food writer should be.

I think James was the first Canadian or perhaps even North American food writer to write at length about sushi and sashimi. Before James, when Japanese food was mentioned in food literature, other elements in Japanese culinary tradition—not sushi and sashimi—were picked up. I believe he was instrumental in popularizing sushi and sashimi in Canada, which is worth noting as these dishes have now become synonymous with Japanese food for many North Americans. It was when he wrote for the *Province* (Vancouver) that sushi and sashimi began to be widely recognized here. And perhaps it was the first time that someone wrote about Japanese cuisine in a mainstream publication. That Japanese food is now so common and popular owes a great deal to James. I believe that he was an epic figure in fostering the growth of the diverse, multicultural food culture of Vancouver.

TOJO'S SAUTÉED BC SPOT PRAWN WITH 21ST-CENTURY SAUCE

Dashi (fish stock), mirin (sweet rice wine), miso (fermented soy bean paste) and yuzu kosho (chili paste) are available in Japanese markets.

¼ cup [50 mL] dashi or chicken stock
2 Tbsp [30 mL] sake
2 Tbsp [30 mL] mirin
2 Tbsp [30 mL] miso
About ¼ tsp [1 mL] yuzu kosho
Dash of canola oil
8 to 10 button mushrooms, halved
1 tsp [5 mL] minced garlic
10 BC spot prawns, heads off, peeled,
   deveined and rinsed
6 asparagus spears, blanched
4 carrots (preferably long, skinny ones),
   peeled and blanched
Pinch of salt and pepper
Chopped scallions

IN A SMALL BOWL, mix the dashi, sake and mirin together, and then whisk in the miso. Whisk in yuzu kosho, adjusting the amount to your preferred spiciness. Set aside.

Heat the canola oil in a frying pan over medium heat and sauté the mushrooms and garlic. When the mushrooms are half cooked, add the prawns. When the prawns are half cooked, pour in the sauce and continue cooking until the prawns turn pink. Take care not to overcook—BC spot prawns cook in a few minutes. Arrange the asparagus and carrots on the plates and place the mushrooms and prawns on top. Season with salt and pepper and garnish with chopped scallions.

TROUT IN CHERMOULA
`2 SERVINGS`

Chermoula is a marinade often used to flavour fish and seafood in North Africa.

4 cloves garlic, finely chopped
1 onion, finely chopped
½ cup [125 mL] chopped cilantro
½ cup [125 mL] olive oil
½ tsp [2 mL] cayenne
½ tsp [2 mL] cumin
½ tsp [2 mL] paprika
½ tsp [2 mL] powdered saffron
½ tsp [2 mL] salt
Juice of a lemon
2 trout, cleaned and dried
All-purpose flour
1 Tbsp [15 mL] vegetable oil
Chopped cilantro

IN A DISH large enough to hold the trout, combine the garlic, onion, cilantro, olive oil, cayenne, cumin, paprika, saffron, salt and lemon juice. Add the trout, rub the mixture into it well and marinate for 1 hour. Remove the trout from the marinade and dredge in flour. In a frying pan over high heat, fry the trout in the vegetable oil for 5 minutes per finger thickness. Stir in the marinade and heat through. Serve the hot marinade over the trout, topped with cilantro.

STEAMED TROUT WITH BLACK BEANS
`2 SERVINGS`

Rainbow trout still glistening with lake water are the best but, in a pinch, farm-raised trout still deliver a great taste.

2 small fresh trout
2 green onions
1 clove garlic, finely chopped
2 Tbsp [30 mL] sherry
2 Tbsp [30 mL] soy sauce
1 Tbsp [15 mL] vegetable oil
2 tsp [10 mL] sugar
1 Tbsp [15 mL] Chinese preserved
  black beans*

SLASH EACH SIDE of the trout diagonally. Slice the green onion diagonally. In a dish large enough to hold the trout, combine the onion with the garlic, sherry, soy sauce, oil and sugar. Marinate the trout in this mixture for 20 minutes. Place the trout on a plate or lettuce leaf in a steamer, scatter the remaining marinade and the black beans over the fish, cover securely and steam for about 8 to 10 minutes. Serve.

*Available at Asian markets.

HALIBUT WITH MANGO MAYONNAISE
`2 SERVINGS`

A blissfully happy marriage of ingredients.

MANGO MAYONNAISE
2 eggs
1 tsp [5 mL] mustard
½ tsp [2 mL] pepper
¼ tsp [1 mL] salt
Juice of 1 lime
½ cup [125 mL] vegetable oil
1 mango, peeled and pitted

COMBINE THE EGGS, mustard, pepper, salt and lime juice in a food processor or blender on medium speed. Slowly pour in the oil in a steady stream and continue processing until the mixture is thick. Add the mango and blend until smooth. Set aside while you prepare the fish.

FISH
2 halibut steaks
1 Tbsp [15 mL] chopped fresh ginger
½ cup [125 mL] lime juice
2 Tbsp [30 mL] vegetable oil

MARINATE THE HALIBUT steaks in the ginger and lime juice for at least 30 minutes. Remove from the marinade. Heat the oil in a frying pan over high heat and cook the steaks for 7 to 8 minutes per finger-thickness of fish. Serve with Mango Mayonnaise.

MEXICAN FISHWIFE FISH
4 SERVINGS

This fish dish is wonderful with rice.

1 lb [500 g] cod fillets
Juice of 1 lemon
2 Tbsp [30 mL] vegetable oil
3 tomatoes, chopped
1 small onion, chopped
1 sweet green pepper, chopped
1 bay leaf
¼ tsp [1 mL] cayenne or chili powder
Pinch of dried thyme
2 Tbsp [30 mL] tomato paste

PLACE THE COD in a dish and pour the lemon juice over the cod. Set aside. Heat the oil in a frying pan over medium-high heat and add the tomato, onion and green pepper. Sauté for 2 to 3 minutes. Reduce the heat to low and add the bay leaf, cayenne and thyme. Cook, covered, for about 20 minutes, until the tomato has collapsed (you should check it a couple of times to make sure the sauce doesn't get too dry). Add the tomato paste to the sauce, stir it in well and then add the fish. Cover and simmer for 5 minutes, remove the cover and simmer for 5 more minutes. Discard the bay leaf. Serve.

FISH WITH HAZELNUT CRUST
2 SERVINGS

2 Tbsp [30 mL] vegetable oil
2 white fish fillets, such as halibut or cod,
   each ⅓ to ½ lb [175–250 g]
1 egg, beaten
½ cup [125 mL] hazelnuts (or any other kind
   of nut), chopped
Zest and juice of 1 lemon
2 Tbsp [30 mL] chopped parsley

HEAT THE OIL in a frying pan over medium heat. Dredge the fish in the beaten egg and sprinkle with chopped hazelnuts. Place the fish in the frying pan and cook for 3 minutes on each side, until the nuts are nice and toasted. Serve with a squeeze of lemon and some parsley and lemon zest sprinkled over top.

FISH WITH BEER AND MUSHROOMS
2 SERVINGS

Originally this recipe used champagne, which seemed fine for a special occasion, even if you couldn't taste the bubbles. One summer evening we caught a lot of lingcod and I cooked them on the dock. We didn't have champagne, we didn't have truffles, we didn't have shallots and we didn't have tarragon. But all sailboats have beer aboard, and somebody else had curry powder. When we got home we improved the recipe with a little cream and dill, but we still remember the way it was before sophistication set in. This is a very pleasant and easy supper for two, though it can easily be expanded for four. When we cook it at home, we serve it with beer in wine glasses.

½ lb [250 g] mushrooms, sliced
1 medium onion, thinly sliced
½ tsp [2 mL] curry powder
3 Tbsp [45 g] butter
1 bottle or can of beer
1 tsp [5 mL] salt
½ tsp [2 mL] pepper
2 cod fillets, each ⅓ to ½ lb [175–250 g]
3 Tbsp [45 mL] whipping cream
3 parsley sprigs, finely chopped
½ tsp [2 mL] green dill, chervil or aniseed
Juice of ½ lemon

IN A FRYING PAN over medium heat, fry the mushrooms with the onion and curry powder in the butter for 5 minutes, stirring frequently. Pour in half of the beer and the salt and pepper. Bring the mixture to a boil. Push the onion and mushrooms to the side of the pan and slide in the fish. Cook, uncovered, for about 3 minutes. Turn the fish carefully and cook for

3 minutes more. Remove the fish from the pan and keep warm. Pour the remaining beer into the pan and boil vigorously for 2 minutes. Add the cream, parsley and dill, and heat through. Sprinkle lemon juice over the fish, pour the sauce over it and serve immediately.

TUNISIAN-SPICED BAKED FISH

2 SERVINGS

Don't start cooking the fish until the doorbell rings. Overcooking fish is what gave it a bad name.

¼ cup [50 mL] olive oil
1½ cups [375 mL] dried bread crumbs
2 cloves garlic, chopped
1 tsp [5 mL] cumin seeds
½ tsp [2 mL] coriander
Pinch of cayenne
2 white fish fillets, such as halibut or cod, each ⅓ to ½ lb [175–250 g]
1 tomato, chopped
Zest and juice of 1 lemon
Handful of basil, chopped
Salt and pepper

PREHEAT OVEN TO 350F [180C]. Heat the oil in a frying pan over high heat. Stir in the bread crumbs, garlic, cumin, coriander and cayenne. Cook until the bread crumbs are crisp and have absorbed all of the oil. Remove from the heat. Place the fish skin-side down in a greased baking dish. Spread the tomato on top of the fish. Sprinkle it with the lemon juice and zest and the basil, and season with salt and pepper. Cover the fish entirely with the bread crumbs. Bake for 15 to 20 minutes. Serve.

FISH WITH PEANUT SAUCE

2 SERVINGS

2 white fish fillets, such as halibut or cod, each ⅓ to ½ lb [175–250 g]
1 lemon, halved
1 Tbsp [15 mL] black pepper
½ tsp [2 mL] salt
2 Tbsp [30 mL] vegetable oil
3 Tbsp [45 mL] Peanut Sauce (page 120)
1 Tbsp [15 mL] vinegar or tamarind juice
Small bunch cilantro

RUB THE FISH with a lemon half and sprinkle the pepper and salt over the fish. Heat the oil in a frying pan. Fry the fish on both sides until three-quarters cooked, about 5 minutes per inch of thickness. Add the peanut sauce and vinegar to the pan. Spoon the liquid over the fish and cook for 2 minutes more. Sprinkle the cilantro on the fish and serve with the remaining lemon, cut into wedges.

AIOLI AND FISH FILLETS

4 SERVINGS

4 fish fillets, each ⅓ to ½ lb [175–250 g]
¼ cup [50 mL] all-purpose flour
1 Tbsp [15 mL] vegetable oil
1 Tbsp [15 mL] butter
Salt and pepper
2 Tbsp [15 mL] chopped parsley
1 cup [250 mL] aioli (page 121)

LIGHTLY DREDGE the fillets in flour. Heat the oil and butter in a frying pan over medium-high heat and fry the fish about 8 minutes per 1 inch of thickness, flipping half way. Season with salt and pepper. Garnish with parsley and serve with aioli.

Recollections of

ROBERT CLARK

EXECUTIVE CHEF, C RESTAURANT, VANCOUVER, BC

To me, James Barber was one of the most genuine and self-assured individuals I have ever met. Most of us adapt to our surroundings and behave appropriately, whereas James travelled through life, creating his own adventures simply by being James Barber.

He made you feel confident in his presence. Through television, he made you feel that anybody could cook. And through his writing, he helped a lot of young chefs and restaurant owners feel that they were a success through their contributions.

A few years ago, I was invited to participate in a Canadian theme dinner at Epcot in Walt Disney World, Florida. James and a few others accompanied me on this expedition into, as far as food culture is concerned, the epic centre of American homogenization and the bastion of blah.

It did not take very long before James had rounded up a posse, including me, to head out in search of something real. Tarpon Springs

on the Gulf of Mexico is where we ended up eating lunch at a quaint little Greek restaurant. Sitting on the patio, savouring a whole red snapper simply roasted with garlic, lemon and olive oil, we all spent a memorable afternoon sharing a wonderful meal. Maybe it was the company, perhaps it was the exceptional fish or maybe, just maybe, it was plain good food, honest and straightforward, which, to me was the essence of James.

At the turn of this century, Pacific sardines began once again showing up on our coast, and they were the first product James offered me advice on. "Salt." That is all he said, and something about wooden barrels during the war. Anyway, for the rest I was on my own.

In August 2007, James was still trying to teach me about sardines as he enthusiastically convinced the guests at Bill Jones's barbecue, how wonderful the charred remains of his grilled sardines tasted.

I have included my most successful sardine dish to date, but James, I am still trying!

89

Robert Clark

ROBERT CLARK'S
BIRCH SYRUP–GLAZED PACIFIC SARDINES

2 SERVINGS

These broiled sardines go great with James's Vegetable Couscous with Mint Salsa (page 100).

Robert Clark

2 Tbsp [30 mL] kosher salt
2 Tbsp [30 mL] sugar
1 tsp [5 mL] ground dill seed
6 whole fresh or frozen Pacific sardines, filleted
2 Tbsp [30 mL] birch syrup (or maple syrup)

COMBINE THE SALT, sugar and ground dill seed. Sprinkle this mixture onto the exposed flesh of the fish and allow to cure in the refrigerator for 5 hours. Rinse off the curing mixture and pat the sardines dry.

Brush the sardines with birch syrup and grill or broil them until the syrup begins to caramelize, about 1 minute.

PASTA & GRAINS

Don't ever cook pasta before guests come; it's worth making them wait. And if you've got any pasta left over, toss it with a little olive oil, a little lemon juice and perhaps half a teaspoon of finely chopped onion and some parsley, and next day (after it sits in fridge all night) you've got a cold salad. —*Flash in the Pan*

TAN TAN NOODLES
2 SERVINGS

1 cup [250 mL] Peanut Sauce (page 120)
1 cup [250 mL] stock or water
3 cups [750 mL] cooked noodles
3 green onions, thinly sliced
Hot chili flakes
Chopped cilantro
Handful of roasted peanuts, chopped

COMBINE THE PEANUT SAUCE and stock in a saucepan and heat until just boiling. Add the noodles. Combine them with the sauce and heat through. Serve sprinkled with green onion, chili flakes, cilantro and peanuts.

DON'T ASK, DON'T TELL QUICK PASTA
2 SERVINGS

Spaghetti doesn't need meatballs. One of my favourites is spaghetti and bread crumbs, a Sicilian, 15-minute quickie that uses dried (but good!) bread, garlic, hot red pepper, olive oil and anchovies. Don't be scared of the anchovies—they disappear into the sauce and nobody knows they're there, but everybody says what a great sauce it is. Don't ask, don't tell! When blood oranges are in season in Sicily, people squeeze a little orange juice over the spaghetti or sprinkle it with a handful of chopped parsley. If you don't have any dried bread, you can use ½ cup [125 mL] packaged bread crumbs. You can also use ¼ cup [50 mL] red wine instead of the orange juice.

2 slices dried bread
Handful of spaghetti
1 tsp [5 mL] olive oil
½ tsp [2 mL] salt
3 Tbsp [45 mL] olive oil
½ tsp [2 mL] red pepper flakes
3 anchovy fillets
1 to 3 cloves garlic, crushed
Juice of half an orange
Olive oil

PUT THE BREAD slices in a plastic bag and roll with a rolling pin or wine bottle until they become fine crumbs. Bring a pot of water to a boil. Add the spaghetti, 1 tsp [5 mL] olive oil and salt. The pasta will be ready in about 7 minutes, which gives you time to make the sauce. Heat a frying pan over medium-high heat. Add 3 Tbsp [45 mL] olive oil and the red pepper flakes, and cook for 1 minute. Add the bread crumbs and cook, stirring vigorously, for 2 minutes. Toss in the anchovies and garlic, and cook for another 2 minutes, mashing with a fork and stirring, until the anchovies are blended in. Pour in the juice, turn up the heat and cook for 2 minutes. Put the spaghetti on plates, the sauce on the spaghetti and a drizzle of olive oil over everything.

PENNE AND POTATOES
4 SERVINGS

This is truly a peasant dish—cheap but tasty and nour-ishing after a hard day's work. The proportions don't matter too much, but the potatoes do. Yukon golds are the best; red potatoes are fine (but you have to watch them carefully); russets don't work at all. Penne is the best pasta for this dish, but any chunky pasta, such as macaroni, is good. Try this dish at home one weekday evening. It's good enough for entertaining, too—just add a green salad and some cheese.

2 Tbsp [30 mL] olive oil
3 medium potatoes, peeled and cut in
   walnut-sized pieces
1 clove garlic, thinly sliced
1 medium onion, thinly sliced
½ tsp [2 mL] pepper
½ tsp [2 mL] salt
1 can [14 oz/398 mL] diced tomatoes
½ tsp [2 mL] oregano
½ tsp [2 mL] red pepper flakes
8 oz [250 g] uncooked penne
   or other large, chunky pasta
Chopped parsley
Grated Parmesan cheese
Extra olive oil (optional)

PLACE THE OIL, potato, garlic, onion, pepper and salt in a cold frying pan. Stir well. Add enough water to cover the onion by ½ inch [1 cm]. Cover and cook on medium-high for about 10 minutes, until the potatoes are almost done but still somewhat firm. Add the tomato with juice, oregano and red pepper flakes. Bring back to a boil, add the pasta and cook, covered, for about 10 minutes, until the pasta is al dente. It should absorb most of the water and may even need an extra ½ cup [125 mL] or so added to keep it moist. Watch the pan carefully for the last couple of minutes, and don't let the pasta stick. Serve sprinkled with parsley, Parmesan and olive oil.

LOVE APPLE FUSILLI
2 SERVINGS

The first tomatoes were bright yellow and were called golden apples. When the red ones evolved, they were often called love apples—Cupid seems to love bright red.

2 Tbsp [30 mL] olive oil
3 cloves garlic, chopped
2 tomatoes, chopped
3 sun-dried tomatoes, chopped

3 sprigs of basil or parsley, chopped
Salt and pepper
3 cups [750 mL] cooked fusilli
½ cup [125 mL] buttermilk
Grated Parmesan cheese

HEAT THE OIL in a frying pan over high heat. Add the garlic and tomato, and cook for 2 to 3 minutes. Add the sun-dried tomato and basil, season with salt and pepper, and cook for 2 to 3 minutes. Stir in the cooked pasta and buttermilk, heat through and serve sprinkled with Parmesan.

FETTUCCINE WITH SPINACH, ZUCCHINI AND WALNUTS
2 SERVINGS

8 oz [250 g] uncooked fettuccine
2 Tbsp [30 mL] vegetable oil
2 cloves garlic, chopped
2 medium zucchini, chopped
1 small onion, chopped
1 bunch spinach, washed and stemmed
Salt and pepper
½ cup [125 g] shredded provolone
   or Monterey Jack cheese
Handful of walnuts, chopped

BRING A LARGE POT of water to a boil and put the pasta on to cook. Meanwhile, heat the oil in a frying pan over medium-high heat. Add the garlic, zucchini and onion. Cook for 4 to 5 minutes, stirring, until the zucchini starts to become transparent. Toss in the spinach, cover, and cook for another 2 minutes. Remove the lid, season the zucchini with salt and pepper, and cook for another 2 minutes, until the water from the spinach evaporates. When the pasta is done, drain it and toss it with the spinach mixture. Serve sprinkled with the provolone and walnuts.

PASTA FAGIOLI

A classic from Tuscany, this pasta dish is dead easy and very comforting.

2 Tbsp [30 ml] olive oil
6 cloves garlic, left whole
3 stalks celery, chopped
2 carrots, chopped
1 red onion, chopped
1 tsp [5 mL] salt
Pinch of pepper
Handful of basil, chopped
1 can [28 oz/796 mL] white beans, rinsed
    and drained
1 cup [250 mL] small pasta (like macaroni)
4 cups [1 L] water or stock
Zest and juice of 1 lemon
½ bunch parsley, chopped
Grated Parmesan cheese

HEAT THE OIL in a large saucepan over medium-high heat. Add the garlic, celery, carrot and onion. Toss the vegetables together, add the salt, pepper and basil, and cook for 3 minutes. Add the beans, pasta and water, bring the mixture to a boil and reduce the heat to low. Simmer for 20 minutes. Stir in the lemon zest and juice. Serve the pasta sprinkled with parsley and Parmesan.

SPICY TURKEY PASTA

This is a great way to use up cooked turkey and left-over pasta. If you have a pickled onion on hand, chop it up and throw it in, too.

1 Tbsp [15 mL] vegetable oil
1 onion, chopped
1 cup [250 mL] cooked turkey meat, cut into
    bite-sized pieces
1 Tbsp [15 mL] chopped parsley
1 tsp [5 mL] cayenne
Freshly ground black pepper
½ sweet red pepper, chopped
2 Tbsp [30 mL] olives
2 cups [500 mL] cooked pasta

HEAT THE OIL in a frying pan over medium heat. Add the onion and cook until transparent. Toss in the turkey meat, parsley, cayenne and black pepper. Stir well. When the mixture is heated through, add the red pepper and olives, and cook for 3 or 4 minutes. Heat the cooked pasta by steaming it in a strainer over boiling water until hot. Tip the pasta onto a plate and top with the spicy turkey mixture.

PORK AND SESAME NOODLES

Ginger and sesame are two of my favourite flavours. For an extra sesame bang, throw a little sesame oil on the noodles at the end. Remember, a little of this oil goes a long way. You can replace the garlic chives in this recipe with ordinary chives and 1 clove garlic, chopped.

2 Tbsp [30 mL] vegetable oil
¾ lb [375 g] pork tenderloin, sliced diagonally
1 onion, chopped
Small bunch garlic chives, chopped
1 tsp [5 mL] chopped fresh ginger
1 Tbsp [15 mL] balsamic vinegar
1 tsp [5 mL] dried chili flakes
1 tsp [5 mL] sugar
Salt and pepper
8 oz [250 g] dried egg noodles
1 Tbsp [15 mL] sesame seeds, toasted
Chopped cilantro or parsley

BRING A LARGE POT of water (for the noodles) to a boil. Heat the oil in a frying pan on high and sauté the pork until lightly browned. Stir in the onion, garlic chives, ginger, vinegar, chili flakes and sugar, and season with salt and pepper. Meanwhile, cook the noodles. When they are done, drain them and toss with the pork mixture and sesame seeds. Serve with cilantro sprinkled on top.

Pasta & Grains

DON GENOVA

FOOD WRITER AND EDUCATOR, FORMER NEIGHBOUR OF JAMES BARBER

*J*ames Barber's cookbook *Flash in the Pan* was the second cookbook I ever owned. I picked it up at a garage sale not long after I moved to Terrace, British Columbia, in 1988. The price on the inside cover was marked at twenty-five cents, but my friends running the garage sale must have sensed my cooking ineptitude and just told me to take it home and use it.

When I was twenty-five, Terrace was the farthest away from home I had ever lived, and it was the first time I went beyond cooking Kraft Dinner and wieners and beans. I hadn't heard of James Barber before that, but I took that little cookbook and started cooking. I cooked everything that caught my interest, circling the recipes on the Contents page as I went along, everything from Chicken and Grapes to Har Tu Fay Kit, his take on a famous northern Chinese beef and spinach dish.

Later, I discovered James on TV with his *Urban Peasant* show. I was working a morning shift at the radio station, which meant I could be home in the afternoon with a notebook and pen, ready to write down the recipes as they unfolded during the half-hour show. Then I went out shopping and cooked them that night for dinner. At the time I had no idea I would eventually become a food journalist, meet James, count him as one of my foodie friends and eventually become his neighbour in the Cowichan Valley. (I even used his old packing boxes when I moved from Vancouver.) We would trade stories about working in television and radio, and he would always grant me a great interview when I needed a story.

I'm looking at that old copy of *Flash in the Pan* as I write this. It is well-stained with food and drink, just the way James would like it. I had forgotten that I had him sign the book for me, and it was a pleasant surprise to reread the inscription: "For Don, with admiration for a really great job. James." That James Barber, someone I greatly admired, liked my work, means a lot to me, and I will try to keep doing a "really great job" in his name.

DON GENOVA'S FETTUCCINE
WITH DUNGENESS CRAB AND WHITE WINE
2 SERVINGS

This recipe was inspired by a lunchtime visit to Clarklewis, a trendy restaurant in an industrial area of Portland, Oregon. I make my own pasta for this recipe, but you can substitute purchased fresh or dried pasta. Use fresh or frozen Dungeness crabmeat if possible, but you could also use a can of lump crabmeat or, to make the dish more economical, a can of crab that has 15 percent leg meat, which will add a bit of texture to the sauce.

> 2 servings of dried or fresh fettuccine
> 1 Tbsp [15 mL] butter
> 1 Tbsp [15 mL] olive oil
> 2 cloves garlic, finely chopped
> 1 cup [250 mL] loosely packed Dungeness crabmeat
>   or 1 can [5 oz/120 g] crabmeat, plus ¼ cup [50 mL]
>   packing liquid
> ¼ to ½ cup [50 to 125 mL] white wine (use the smaller
>   amount if using canned crab)
> 1 tsp [5 mL] hot pepper flakes
> Salt and freshly ground black pepper
> 2 Tbsp [30 mL] chopped parsley

BOIL THE WATER for the pasta and, while the pasta is cooking, make the sauce.

Heat the butter and olive oil in a large sauté pan and cook the garlic over medium heat. When the garlic has softened, add the crabmeat, reserved packing liquid (if using), white wine and hot pepper flakes. Bring to a simmer. When the pasta is ready, drain it and add it to the sauce in the pan. Stir to coat the pasta. Place the pasta on warm plates and top with salt, pepper and parsley. Enjoy!

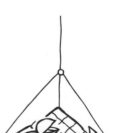

PASTA WITH SAUSAGE AND PRAWNS

2 SERVINGS

2 Tbsp [30 mL] vegetable oil
3 cloves garlic, chopped
1 small onion, chopped
2 tomatoes, chopped
1 spicy Italian sausage, sliced into bite-sized
    pieces
1 sweet red pepper, chopped
½ cup [125 mL] red wine
8 oz [250 g] uncooked pasta, such as rigatoni
    or penne
8 fresh prawns, rinsed, peeled and deveined
Salt and pepper
Handful of parsley, chopped

BRING A LARGE POT of water (for the pasta) to a boil. Heat the oil in a saucepan over medium-high heat. Add the garlic and onion, and cook for 2 to 3 minutes, until the onion starts to become transparent. Toss in the tomato and cook for 3 minutes. Add the sausage and red pepper, and cook for 2 minutes. Pour in the wine, reduce the heat to low, cover the saucepan and simmer the sausage mixture for about 15 minutes. Meanwhile, add the pasta to the boiling water and cook for 8 to 10 minutes, until al dente. Stir the prawns into the sausage mixture and cook for 2 minutes, or until the prawns just turn pink. Drain the pasta. Season the sauce with salt and pepper and serve over the drained pasta, sprinkled with parsley.

SPAGHETTINI WITH CLAMS, BURNT BUTTER AND LEMON
2 SERVINGS

This dish is still tremendous without the fresh clams— just reduce the wine, lemon juice and juice from the canned clams by one-third by simmering the sauce for about 10 minutes before adding the canned clams.

1 lb [500 g] small fresh clams in the shell
2 Tbsp [30 mL] butter
½ medium onion, finely chopped
½ cup [125 mL] white wine
1 Tbsp [15 mL] fresh lemon juice
1 can [5 oz/142 g] clams with juice
Handful of spaghettini
Handful of parsley, finely chopped
2 Tbsp [30 mL] grated Parmesan cheese

CLEAN THE FRESH CLAMS by brushing the shells under cold running water. Discard any that are not tightly closed. Bring a large pot of water (for the pasta) to a boil. Heat the butter in a frying pan over high heat until it begins to brown. Reduce the heat to low, add the onion and cook until soft. Add the fresh clams, wine, lemon juice and juice from the canned clams. Bring the mixture to a boil. Cover the saucepan, reduce the heat and simmer for about 5 minutes. Discard any clams that do not open. Add the pasta to the boiling water and the canned clams and parsley to the sauce. Keep the sauce warm over low heat until the pasta is cooked al dente. Drain the pasta and toss with the sauce. Serve immediately with Parmesan.

PUTTANESCA SAUCE
MAKES ABOUT 2 CUPS [500 ML]

This sauce is wonderful with many types of pasta.

1 Tbsp [15 mL] vegetable oil
1 onion, chopped
6 anchovy fillets
6 tomatoes, chopped
2 cloves garlic, chopped
2 Tbsp [30 mL] water
1 Tbsp [15 mL] tomato paste
Bay leaf
2 Tbsp [30 mL] chopped black olives
1 Tbsp [15 mL] capers
1 Tbsp [15 mL] vinegar
Freshly ground pepper

HEAT THE OIL in a frying pan over medium heat. Brown the onion. Toss in the anchovies and mash until they are blended in. Add the tomato, garlic, water, tomato paste and bay leaf. Bring the mixture to a boil, reduce the heat and simmer for 10 minutes. Add the olives, capers, vinegar and pepper, and stir until everything is heated through. Remove the bay leaf. Toss just-cooked pasta with the sauce. Serve immediately.

PASTA CON LE SARDE (PASTA WITH SARDINES)

This is another delicious sauce for any type of pasta.

    4 servings of uncooked pasta
    4 fresh sardines
    All-purpose flour
    4 Tbsp [60 mL] olive oil
    1 fennel bulb, chopped
    1 onion, chopped
    1 Tbsp [15 mL] all-purpose flour
    1 can anchovy fillets
    2 Tbsp [30 mL] almonds or walnuts, toasted
    2 Tbsp [30 mL] sultanas
    2 Tbsp [30 mL] chopped parsley
    1 Tbsp [15 mL] vinegar
    Salt and pepper
    4 Tbsp [60 mL] fried bread crumbs

BRING A LARGE pot pot of water (for the pasta) to a boil. Dredge the sardines in flour. Heat 2 Tbsp of the oil in a frying pan. Fry the sardines until crisp and brown. Set them aside on a plate and keep warm. Meanwhile, add the pasta to the boiling water and cook until *al dente*. Heat the remainder of the oil in the frying pan and brown the fennel and onion. Sprinkle with 1 Tbsp [15 mL] flour, add the anchovies and stir vigorously until they are blended in. Add the nuts, sultanas, parsley and vinegar. Season with salt and pepper and cook for 2 minutes, until the sultanas have plumped up. Toss just-cooked pasta with the sauce. Arrange the sardines on top and sprinkle with the bread crumbs. Serve immediately.

PASTA FRITTATA

Whether served hot or cold, this frittata is a great recipe for using up cooked pasta.

    ¼ cup [50 mL] butter
    1 green pepper, chopped
    1 onion, chopped
    1 cup [250 mL] sliced mushrooms
    6 eggs
    1 cup [250 mL] milk
    1 cup [250 mL] shredded cheese, such as cheddar
    1 Tbsp [15 mL] chopped basil
    Handful of parsley, chopped
    Salt and pepper
    2 cups [500 mL] cooked pasta
    2 Tbsp [30 mL] grated Parmesan cheese

PREHEAT OVEN TO 375F [190C]. Melt the butter in an ovenproof frying pan over medium heat. Add the green pepper, onion and mushrooms, and cook for 2 to 3 minutes. In a large bowl, beat the eggs with the milk. Stir in the cheese, basil and parsley, and season with salt and pepper. Combine the cooked pasta with the vegetables in the frying pan and immediately pour the egg mixture over top. Cover the pan with an ovenproof lid, place the pan in the oven and bake for 15 minutes, until the eggs are almost set and the frittata has puffed up. Remove the pan from the oven and turn on the broiler. Sprinkle grated Parmesan on the frittata and broil, uncovered, until the top is browned, about 2 minutes. Slice and serve.

LEMON-SCENTED RICE

    2 cups [500 mL] water
    Pinch of salt
    1 cup [250 mL] long-grain rice
    3 Tbsp [45 mL] butter
    Zest and juice of 1 lemon

IN A SAUCEPAN, bring the water to a boil with the salt. Add the rice and return to a boil. Cover, lower the heat and simmer for 20 minutes. Remove the lid and stir in the butter and the lemon zest and juice.

BACHELOR'S FRIED RICE
4 SIDE-DISH OR 2 MAIN-COURSE SERVINGS

2 Tbsp [30 mL] vegetable oil
2 onions, finely chopped
Pepper
4 mushrooms, thinly sliced
2 cloves garlic, chopped
1 can [7 oz/196 mL] shrimp, rinsed and drained
3 cups [750 mL] cooked rice
½ cup [125 mL] green peas
2 Tbsp [30 mL] turmeric
2 Tbsp [30 mL] water
Handful of bean sprouts
1 egg, beaten
2 green onions, cut into 1-inch [2.5 cm] lengths

HEAT THE OIL in a large frying pan over medium heat. Add the onion and lots of pepper, and cook for 2 to 3 minutes. Toss in the mushrooms and garlic, and cook a further 2 to 3 minutes. Add the shrimp, rice, peas, turmeric, water and bean sprouts; stir well and cook for 5 minutes. Pour the egg over top of the rice mixture and stir until the egg has cooked, about 2 minutes. Sprinkle with green onions and serve immediately.

COCONUT RICE
2 SERVINGS

½ cup [125 mL] coconut milk
¾ cup [175 mL] cold water
1 clove garlic
2 green onions
½-inch [1 cm] piece fresh ginger
Few sprigs of thyme
½ cup [125 mL] long-grain rice, rinsed
¼ tsp [1 mL] salt

PUT THE COCONUT MILK in a saucepan with the cold water and bring to a boil. Meanwhile, peel the garlic and smash it flat with the broad side of a knife. Cut the green onions into three lengths and smash them as well. Cut the ginger into two slices large enough to be easily spotted and removed when the rice is finished. Remove the thyme leaves from the stalks. Add the garlic, onion, ginger, thyme, rice and salt to the boiling coconut milk and return to a boil. Reduce the heat, cover and simmer for 15 minutes, or until all the liquid has been absorbed. Discard the garlic and ginger, and serve.

VEGETABLE COUSCOUS WITH MINT SALSA
4 SERVINGS

VEGETABLE COUSCOUS
2 cups [500 mL] water
1 cup [250 mL] couscous
2 Tbsp [30 mL] olive oil
2 tomatoes, chopped
1 carrot, chopped
1 onion, chopped
½ tsp [2 mL] curry powder
½ tsp [2 mL] salt
1 apple, cored and chopped

BRING THE WATER to a boil in a small saucepan over high heat. Pour in the couscous, cover and turn the heat off. Let stand for 5 minutes, until the couscous has absorbed all the water.

Heat the oil in a frying pan over medium-high heat. Add the tomatoes, carrot, onion, curry powder and salt, and cook for 3 to 4 minutes, until the onion has softened and the tomatoes start to collapse. Add the apple and remove from heat.

SALSA
1 bunch fresh mint, stems removed
2 Tbsp [30 mL] cider vinegar
1 Tbsp [15 mL] honey

PURÉE THE MINT with the vinegar and honey in a small food processor or spice mill until a smooth paste forms. Put the couscous onto a serving plate and top with the vegetable mixture and salsa. Serve.

POLENTA MAMAGLIA
4 SERVINGS

Polenta is one of my favourite foods on a cold winter day. Garnish it with crumbled feta cheese, black olives, pickles, grilled green onions or fennel, hard-boiled eggs, roasted red peppers or fresh herbs.

3 cups [750 mL] water
½ tsp [2 mL] salt
1 cup [250 mL] yellow cornmeal
2 Tbsp [30 mL] butter, melted

PLACE THE WATER and salt in large saucepan and bring to a boil over high heat. Pour in the cornmeal in a steady stream, stirring continuously. Reduce the heat to low and cook for 15 to 20 minutes, stirring to prevent lumps. Pour the polenta onto a large platter, shape into a mound and pour the melted butter over top.

QUINOA WITH MINT AND FETA
4 SERVINGS

1 cup [250 mL] quinoa
2 cups [500 mL] boiling water or stock
1 tsp [5 mL] salt
½ onion, finely chopped
1 cup [250 mL] crumbled feta cheese
½ cup [125 mL] chopped mint
2 to 3 Tbsp [30–45 mL] olive oil
Salt and pepper

WASH AND DRAIN the quinoa. Place in a saucepan with the boiling water and salt. Bring to a boil, reduce the heat, cover and simmer until the liquid has been absorbed, about 10 minutes. Fluff the quinoa with a fork and add the onion, feta, mint, olive oil and some salt and pepper. Toss well and serve.

ASIAN ALMOST RISOTTO
3 TO 4 SERVINGS

More fuss is made over risotto than needs to be. Gourmet magazines go on and on with far too many details, each of which may indeed make a very slight difference to the final product. But risotto (which, among other things, Napoleon's chef is supposed to have discovered on the way to Moscow) is basically peasant food—quick and simple. This recipe is essentially a make-it-up-as-you-go dish. You can add sliced mushrooms with the meat, or chopped sweet red peppers, and you can stir in a handful of chopped greens (lettuce or cabbage leaves) for the last 2 minutes of cooking. One of my children uses Spam for the meat in this dish, which I (on principle) object to, but it's so good I can't turn it down. Just use a bit less soy sauce in the Spam version.

2 Tbsp [30 mL] vegetable oil
¼ cup [50 mL] water
10 thin slices fresh ginger
2 cloves garlic, chopped
1 onion, chopped
1 tsp [5 mL] pepper
1 cup [250 mL] cubed cooked chicken or
    pork
1 cup [250 mL] rice (not instant)
1 cup [250 mL] stock or 1 chicken stock cube
    dissolved in 1 cup [250 mL] boiling water
1 cup [250 mL] water, or half water, half wine
Soy sauce or oyster sauce

HEAT THE OIL and ¼ cup [50 mL] water in a frying pan over medium heat. Add the ginger, garlic, onion and pepper, and cook for 4 minutes. Toss in the meat and heat for 2 minutes. Stir in the rice, mixing well. Add stock and bring to a boil; stir well and add the remaining water. Simmer, covered, for 12 minutes. Turn off the heat, let the rice stand for 3 minutes, sprinkle with a little soy sauce and serve.

> I never defrost frozen peas, just dump them straight into the dish, unless I put an ounce of butter in a small saucepan, line it with lettuce leaves, dump in the peas, sprinkle with salt and pepper and a good half-teaspoon of dried mint (or some fresh mint leaves), put on the lid and cook at medium heat, shaking frequently, for 6 or 7 minutes. —*Fear Of Frying*

EXOTIC PILAF
6 TO 8 SERVINGS

4 Tbsp [60 mL] butter
1 cup [250 mL] rice
1 cup [250 mL] water
1½ cups [375 mL] white wine
1 cup [250 mL] almonds
1 cup [250 mL] dried apricots, chopped
1 cup [250 mL] prunes, chopped
1 cup [250 mL] raisins
½ cup [125 mL] dates, chopped
½ cup [125 mL] dried figs, chopped
½ tsp [2 mL] cinnamon
½ tsp [2 mL] salt
¼ tsp [1 mL] cloves
Juice of ½ lemon

MELT 1 TBSP [15 ML] of the butter in a frying pan and add the rice, stirring until all of it is covered with butter. Pour in the water and 1 cup [250 mL] of the white wine. Cover and simmer for 15 to 20 minutes. Meanwhile, melt the remaining butter in a large frying pan and toss in the almonds. When browned, add the apricots, prunes, raisins, dates, figs, cinnamon, salt and cloves, and stir until well combined. Pour in the remaining white wine and the lemon juice. Pile the rice onto a platter and the fruit mixture on top.

PISELLI A TORTINO (PEA CAKE)
2 SERVINGS

2 Tbsp [30 mL] olive oil
1 clove garlic, chopped
1 onion, chopped
2 cups [500 mL] cooked rice
2 cups [500 mL] green peas
1 Tbsp [15 mL] chopped mint
Salt and pepper
3 eggs, beaten
3 Tbsp [45 mL] grated Parmesan cheese

PREHEAT THE OVEN to 400F [200C]. Heat the oil in a frying pan over high heat, add the garlic and onion, and cook for 2 to 3 minutes, until softened. Stir in the rice, peas and mint, and season with salt and pepper. Remove from the heat after 1 minute and stir in the eggs and Parmesan. Pour the rice mixture into a greased baking dish and bake for 20 to 25 minutes.

> One-pot suppers are the salvation of the two-job marriage.
> —*Mushrooms Are Marvellous*

VEGETABLES

GRILLED LEEKS

2 SERVINGS

This side dish is perfect for making in the toaster oven.

6 leeks
1 Tbsp [15 mL] sesame oil
2 Tbsp [30 mL] soy sauce
Pinch of cayenne pepper

TURN ON THE BROILER. Cut the leeks into finger lengths and brush with the sesame oil. Broil until they are browned. In a small bowl, mix the soy sauce and cayenne pepper and brush the mixture over the leeks. Return to the broiler and cook for about 10 minutes, until tender.

CARROT KIMPURA

2 SERVINGS

Don't be daunted at the thought of preparing Japanese food. Because of the traditional scarcity of fuel in Japan, Japanese food for the most part requires only fast cooking. It's the best fast food around. Mirin is available in Japanese markets and many grocery stores. If you don't have mirin, you can substitute 1 Tbsp [15 mL] white wine plus 1 tsp [5 mL] sugar. Serve this carrot dish hot or cold.

3 carrots
2 Tbsp [30 mL] vinegar
½ tsp [2 mL] salt
Pepper
3 hot red chili peppers
2 Tbsp [30 mL] olive oil
1 Tbsp [15 mL] sugar
3 Tbsp [45 mL] soy sauce
1 Tbsp [15 mL] mirin
1 Tbsp [15 mL] sake or whiskey
1 Tbsp [15 mL] toasted sesame seeds

CUT THE CARROTS into matchsticks. In a bowl, combine the vinegar, salt and pepper; add the carrots and soak for 10 minutes. Remove the carrots

from the vinegar mixture and dry them. Heat the chili peppers in a dry frying pan over high heat until they start to smoke. Add the carrots and oil, and stir well. Add the sugar, pour in the soy sauce, mirin and sake, and boil the mixture until the carrots are glazed. Tip them onto a plate and sprinkle with toasted sesame seeds.

OH BABY BABY ARTICHOKES

2 SERVINGS

Whenever you find baby artichokes at the market, buy them. They're hard to find but so good.

8 to 10 baby artichokes
Juice of 1 lemon
2 Tbsp [30 mL] olive oil
6 cloves garlic, chopped
1 Tbsp [15 mL] pepper
½ tsp [2 mL] salt

REMOVE THE OUTER LEAVES of the artichokes and trim the stalks. Place them in a bowl of water with a little of the lemon juice. Heat the oil in a frying pan, drain the artichokes and cut them in half and place them, cut side down, in a single layer in the pan. Add the garlic and pepper. Cover the pan and cook until the bottoms of the artichokes have browned. Sprinkle them with salt, pour some lemon juice over them and serve.

SICILIAN PUMPKIN WITH MINT

2 SERVINGS

2 Tbsp [30 mL] vegetable oil
½ lb [250 g] pumpkin or squash, cut into
    ½-inch (1 cm) thick pieces
1 clove garlic, chopped
Pinch of white sugar
Sprig of mint, chopped
Salt and pepper

HEAT THE OIL in a frying pan over medium-high heat. Add the pumpkin and cook for 6 minutes. Turn the slices of pumpkin over, and add the garlic and sugar. Cook for 6 more minutes, until the pumpkin is tender and cooked through. Sprinkle with the mint, season with some salt and pepper, and serve.

"PASTA" AND GOAT CHEESE

4 SERVINGS

Spaghetti squash is really a fun discovery. I use it with just about any pasta sauce.

1 spaghetti squash, halved
1 Tbsp [15 mL] butter
1 Tbsp [15 mL] olive oil
4 cloves garlic, finely chopped
½ cup [125 mL] chopped walnuts
Handful of chopped parsley
½ cup [125 mL] cream
4 oz [125 g] goat cheese
2 Tbsp [30 mL] grated Parmesan cheese
Handful of chopped basil
Salt and pepper

BRING A LARGE POT of water to a boil and cook the spaghetti squash for 15 minutes, or until tender. Drain. Pull out the spaghetti-like strands of the squash with a fork. Melt the butter with the oil in a frying pan and sauté the garlic, walnuts and parsley. Remove the walnut mixture from the pan. In a bowl, combine the cream, goat cheese and Parmesan. Toss the spaghetti squash with the walnut and cheese mixtures, and sprinkle with basil, salt and pepper. Serve hot.

BAKED SWEET-POTATO FRENCH FRIES

2 TO 4 SERVINGS

2 sweet potatoes or yams
Vegetable oil
Cayenne pepper
Salt and pepper

PREHEAT OVEN TO 400F [200C]. Cut the sweet potatoes into small wedges and place them in a greased baking dish or sheet. Drizzle the wedges with oil, sprinkle with cayenne, salt and pepper, and bake, uncovered, for 25 to 30 minutes, or until crispy on the outside, tender on the inside.

When you cook potatoes or rice, always make twice as much as you'll need. Next day you make fish cakes or shepherd's pie, or you mix 'em up with an egg and fry them for breakfast.
—Fear Of Frying

MASHED POTATOES

USING A FORK, mash the potatoes with lots of pepper, some salt, 1 Tbsp [15 mL] butter per potato and some parsley. Don't add milk or cream, and don't be shy about leaving a few small lumps. Be generous with the pepper.

ROSEMARY POTATOES

3 SERVINGS

Rosemary and potatoes have a natural affinity for each other.

1 lb [500 g] potatoes, cut into pieces
   just too big for a mouthful
4 Tbsp [60 mL] olive oil
4 cloves garlic, chopped
2 Tbsp [30 mL] chopped parsley
2 Tbsp [30 mL] chopped rosemary
   or 1 ½ tsp [7 mL] dried
Salt and pepper

PREHEAT OVEN TO 400F [200C]. Place the potatoes in a baking dish. Drizzle the oil over them and sprinkle on the garlic, parsley, rosemary and some salt and pepper. Bake for 20 minutes, or until brown and crisp.

The Genius of James Barber

British children learn at their mothers' knees to cook cabbage. Not just to cook it, but to destroy it—to give it a terrible reputation and make an international joke of it. But out of this soggy, tasteless mess they also learn to make a most magnificent dish called Bubble and Squeak, which when properly made is as close as the British will ever come to soul food.

Making authentic Bubble and Squeak requires lamb left over from the Sunday roast and cold cooked potatoes from the same meal. Also quantities of leftover cooked cabbage, and that it be Monday, and that it be cooked by a mum. —*Flash in the Pan*

BUBBLE AND SQUEAK
2 SERVINGS

This classic British dish made with leftovers squeaks and bubbles as it cooks.

¼ cup [50 mL] butter
1 egg, beaten
2 cups [500 mL] chopped cooked cabbage
2 cups [500 mL] mashed cooked potato
1 Tbsp [15 mL] pepper

MELT THE BUTTER in a frying pan over medium heat. In a large bowl, combine the egg, cabbage, potato and pepper. Place the mixture in the frying pan and pat down into a cake. Reduce the heat to low and cook until the bottom has browned, about 15 minutes. Invert a plate on top of the frying pan and flip the cake onto the plate. Eat just as is, or slip the cake back into the frying pan and cook the other side for 2 to 3 minutes before serving.

POTATOES WITH WALNUTS AND YOGURT
3 SERVINGS

2 large potatoes, cut into bite-sized pieces
Handful of walnuts
½ cup [125 mL] yogurt
Few sprigs of cilantro
Salt and pepper

PUT THE POTATOES on to boil. Meanwhile, toast the walnuts in a dry frying pan over high heat. Let them cool and then chop them. When the potatoes are done, drain them and toss them immediately with the walnuts and yogurt. Tear the cilantro leaves into coarse pieces and sprinkle them over the potatoes. Season with salt and pepper and serve.

POTATOES STEAMED IN BUTTERMILK
3 SERVINGS

2 cups [500 mL] buttermilk
1 lb [500 g] potatoes, peeled
Salt and pepper
Butter
½ cup [125 mL] toasted oatmeal (optional)

HEAT THE BUTTERMILK in a saucepan and add the potatoes. Sprinkle with salt and lots of pepper; cover and simmer until the potatoes are tender, about 15 minutes. Serve with a knob of butter and sprinkled with toasted oatmeal (if using).

TOMATADA
3 SERVINGS

1 lb [500 g] small potatoes, with skins
2 Tbsp [30 mL] olive oil
2 to 3 cloves garlic, chopped
½ onion, chopped
2 Tbsp [30 mL] white wine
1 tsp [5 mL] tomato paste
Chopped parsley

BOIL THE POTATOES and drain, dry and slice them. Heat the oil over medium-high heat and fry the potato slices until golden brown on each side. Mix in the garlic, onion, wine and tomato paste. Stir until the potato slices are well coated with the tomato mixture. Add the parsley, stir and serve.

SPICY POTATO PANCAKES
MAKES ABOUT 1 DOZEN 3-INCH [7.5 CM] PANCAKES

2 Tbsp [30 mL] vegetable oil
2 eggs
1 onion, grated
1 lb [500 g] baking potatoes, peeled, grated and squeezed dry
½ cup [125 mL] all-purpose flour
½ tsp [2 mL] turmeric
Bunch of chives, chopped
Pinch of cayenne pepper
Salt and pepper
1 tsp [5 mL] cumin seeds

HEAT THE OIL in a frying pan over medium heat. In a bowl, combine the eggs, onion, potato, flour, turmeric, chives and cayenne to form a thick mixture. Season with salt and pepper. Add the cumin seeds to the pan and cook for 30 seconds. Add large spoonfuls of the potato mixture to the pan, flattening with a spatula to form round cakes. Cook for 3 to 4 minutes, until golden. Turn and cook for 2 minutes more.

PARSNIP, POTATO AND GINGER SOUFFLÉ
4 SERVINGS

Everyone seems to have forgotten about the joys of soufflé.

2 cups [500 mL] mashed cooked parsnip
1 cup [250 mL] mashed cooked potato
½ cup [125 mL] milk or cream
3 Tbsp [45 mL] butter
2 tsp [10 mL] grated ginger
1 tsp [5 mL] black pepper
½ tsp [2 mL] salt
Zest of ½ lemon or orange
3 eggs, separated

PREHEAT OVEN TO 350F [180C]. In a large bowl, beat together the parsnip and potato with the milk, butter, ginger, pepper, salt and lemon zest until fluffy. Beat in the egg yolks. In a separate bowl, whip the egg whites until stiff and fold them into the parsnip mixture. Pour into a medium-sized greased soufflé dish and bake for 30 to 40 minutes.

PROVENÇAL BAKED VEGETABLES
4 SERVINGS

Just throw it together, bung it in the oven and put up your feet.

2 tomatoes, sliced
1 medium-sized eggplant, sliced
1 medium-sized zucchini, sliced
1 onion, sliced
4 cloves garlic, chopped
1 cup [250 mL] shredded mozzarella cheese
¼ cup [50 mL] grated Parmesan cheese
1 tsp [5 mL] chopped basil
1 tsp [5 mL] chopped oregano
Salt and pepper
3 Tbsp [45 mL] olive oil

PREHEAT OVEN TO 350F [180C]. Grease an ovenproof dish and place alternating slices of tomato, eggplant, zucchini and onion in the dish. Sprinkle with the garlic, mozzarella, Parmesan, basil and oregano, and season with salt and pepper. Drizzle the oil over top and bake for 25 to 30 minutes, or until the cheese is bubbling and browned and the vegetables have softened.

Rutabagas, those big old yellow old turnips that nobody buys (they keep them in the supermarkets just to confuse the cost-of-living index) are badly neglected. Eat them raw in thin strips with soy sauce, or mash them with an equal quantity of mashed potatoes, lots of butter and maybe a beaten egg, lots of pepper and some salt. Enjoy enjoy enjoy. —*Fear Of Frying*

EGGPLANT GRILLED WITH MOZZARELLA

CRISP-FRY THICK SLICES of eggplant. Lay mozzarella slices over half the eggplant slices and sprinkle with some chopped garlic and freshly ground pepper. Top with another slice of eggplant and broil the eggplant sandwich until the mozzarella just melts, about 2 or 3 minutes. Serve.

TURKISH EGGPLANT SANDWICHES
2 SERVINGS

¼ cup [50 mL] vegetable oil
2 oz [50 g] feta cheese
4 slices eggplant, each ½-inch (1 cm) thick
¼ cup [50 mL] bread crumbs
1 egg

HEAT THE OIL in a frying pan over medium-high heat. Crumble half of the cheese over one slice of eggplant. Place another slice of eggplant on top, to make a sandwich. Place the bread crumbs in a shallow dish, and beat the egg in another shallow dish until it is uniform in colour. Dip the sandwich in the egg and then in the bread crumbs, coating both sides. Place the sandwich in the frying pan. Repeat with the remaining ingredients. Cook the sandwiches for 4 to 5 minutes on each side, until the cheese has melted and the eggplant is cooked. Serve immediately.

SPICY CHINESE EGGPLANT
4 SERVINGS

3 Tbsp [45 mL] vegetable oil
½ onion, chopped
2 to 3 Asian eggplants, cut into chunks

5 to 6 whole hot peppers
½ sweet green pepper, chopped
½ sweet red pepper, chopped
1 Tbsp [15 mL] black bean sauce
1 Tbsp [15 mL] soy sauce
1 tsp [5 mL] tomato paste
½ tsp [2 mL] salt
½ tsp [2 mL] sugar
1 tsp [5 mL] sesame oil

HEAT THE OIL in a frying pan over high heat and sauté the onion until transparent. Toss in the eggplant and sauté until evenly coloured. Add the hot and sweet peppers, black bean sauce, soy sauce, tomato paste, salt and sugar, and continue to cook, stirring, on high heat for 5 to 6 minutes. Stir in the sesame oil and serve.

CURRIED MUSHROOMS
4 SERVINGS

2 Tbsp [30 mL] butter
¼ medium onion, chopped
1 garlic clove, chopped
½ tsp [2 mL] curry powder
½ lb [250 g] mushrooms, sliced
½ tsp [2 mL] salt
Juice of ½ lemon
3 Tbsp [45 mL] heavy cream

MELT THE BUTTER in a frying pan over medium heat and cook the onion until it is transparent. Stir in the garlic and curry powder. Add the mushrooms, salt and lemon juice, stir well and cook for 5 minutes. Pour in the cream and cook the mushroom mixture for 2 minutes more. Serve hot or cold.

Recollections of

BERGLIND KRISTINSDOTTIR

MARKETING ASSISTANT

110

Berglind Kristinsdottir

I experienced ratatouille of a different flavour with James Barber.

It was probably the hottest day of the year when I picked up James in my cramped black hatchback at the start of his Vancouver book tour for the new edition of *Cooking for Two*. It was before eight o'clock in the morning and I hadn't yet put food in my stomach when James insisted we go for breakfast at a small Middle Eastern café in Gastown. Not fully understanding the legend in my midst, I declined his eager recommendation to order the most spicy, meaty, tomatoey stew on the menu. This was when the "Urban Peasant" made it his mission to make me more familiar with urban food. Our whirlwind book tour developed into a whirlwind food tour that led us through the markets of Chinatown and Granville Island, inside the best Chinese restaurant in the city and to the best cup of coffee Vancouver had to offer. With our bellies full and his book launch still four hours away, James was ready for a siesta at his Gastown apartment. When we realized he was exiled without a key, we needed to find a different escape from the unrelenting summer heat. As James flipped through a newspaper over his cup of coffee, he discovered the movie listings. Soon we were settling into our seats at Tinseltown theatre to watch the animated film *Ratatouille*. The cartoon rats shared James's passion for cooking and seemed to strike a chord with the old foodie, who truly believed that everyone can and should cook.

I never had the chance to taste James Barber's ratatouille, but I could not be more satisfied with the unconventional version we shared together.

RATATOUILLE

4 SERVINGS

The French classic in under half an hour.

¼ cup [50 mL] olive oil
3 medium-sized zucchinis, chopped
2 tomatoes, chopped
1 medium-sized eggplant, chopped
1 onion, chopped
3 cloves garlic, left whole
1 Tbsp [15 mL] tomato paste
1 tsp [5 mL] chopped basil
1 tsp [5 mL] chopped oregano
½ cup [125 mL] water
Salt and pepper
Handful of chopped parsley

HEAT THE OIL in a saucepan over high heat. Stir in the zucchini, tomato, eggplant and onion. When the vegetables are coated in oil, stir in the garlic, tomato paste, basil and oregano. Pour in the water, cover and reduce the heat to medium-low. Simmer for 25 to 30 minutes, or until all the vegetables are well cooked. Season with salt and pepper, sprinkle with parsley and serve.

FRIED GREEN TOMATOES

2 SERVINGS

Fried tomatoes are the perfect complement to a bacon-and-eggs breakfast.

3 to 4 slices bacon
½ cup [125 mL] all-purpose flour
1 tsp [5 mL] oregano
½ tsp [2 mL] salt
½ tsp [2 mL] pepper
2 green tomatoes

IN A FRYING PAN, fry the bacon until crisp. Remove the bacon from the pan and reserve. In a small bowl, combine the flour, oregano, salt and pepper. Cut the tomatoes into thick slices and dip them in the flour mixture. Fry the tomatoes in the bacon fat and serve.

GARLIC VEGETABLE SAUTÉ

2 SERVINGS

In a tiny bar in a little Greek village without electricity, we ate this dish with fresh mussels right off the beach. It goes well with noodles.

10 cloves garlic, unpeeled
3 Tbsp [45 mL] olive oil
1 sweet green pepper, sliced
1 sweet red pepper, sliced
1 zucchini, sliced
1 tsp [5 mL] thyme
Salt and pepper
2 Tbsp [30 mL] crumbled feta cheese

PREHEAT OVEN TO 300F [150C]. Place the garlic on a baking sheet, drizzle with a bit of the olive oil and roast in the oven for about 30 minutes. When done, heat the remaining oil in a large frying pan and sauté the peppers and zucchini for 2 minutes. Pop the garlic cloves out of their skins and stir into the vegetables. Stir in the thyme, season the pepper mixture with salt and pepper, and sprinkle with feta.

BEANS TOSCANA

4 SERVINGS

Cannellini beans, used in Italian cuisine, are large white beans similar to kidney beans.

¾ cup [175 mL] cannellini beans, soaked overnight
2 cloves garlic, chopped
2 tomatoes, chopped
1 onion, finely chopped
1 can [7 oz/198 g] tuna
2 Tbsp [30 mL] chopped parsley
2 Tbsp [30 mL] olive oil
1 tsp [5 mL] chopped oregano
½ tsp [2 mL] salt
Juice of ½ lemon
Cherry tomatoes

RINSE AND DRAIN the beans. Place them in a large saucepan with plenty of water and bring to a boil. Cover and simmer for about 45 minutes, or until tender. Drain the beans and place them in a bowl. Add the garlic, tomato, onion, tuna, parsley, olive oil, oregano, salt and lemon juice, and toss until the ingredients are well combined. Garnish with cherry tomatoes and serve.

PAN HAGGERTY

2 SERVINGS

A coal miner's supper from northeast England.

3 Tbsp [45 mL] vegetable oil
3 small potatoes, thinly sliced
1 small onion, thinly sliced
½ cup [125 g] shredded cheddar cheese

HEAT 2 TBSP [30 ML] of the oil in a frying pan over medium-high heat. Reduce the heat to low, lay one-third of the potato slices in the bottom of the pan and one-third of the onion slices on top of them. Sprinkle with half of the cheese. Repeat with another third of each of the potato and onion. Sprinkle with the remaining cheese. Top with the remaining onion and then the potato. Cook, covered, for 20 to 25 minutes. Remove the lid and invert a plate over the frying pan. Flip the potato mixture onto the plate so that the cooked side is up. Add the remaining oil to the pan and slide the potato mixture back into it. Cook for 10 minutes, covered. Serve.

ZUCCHINI LATKES

2 SERVINGS

2 zucchinis, grated (about 2 cups/500 mL)
1 Tbsp [15 mL] all-purpose flour
1 tsp [5 mL] pepper
1 tsp [5 mL] tarragon
1 egg
2 Tbsp [30 mL] olive oil
3 Tbsp [45 mL] yogurt
1 tsp [5 mL] tomato paste
Juice of ½ lemon

IN A BOWL, combine the zucchini, flour, pepper and tarragon. Mix in the egg. Fry the latkes in batches: heat half the oil in a frying pan over medium heat and put mounded tablespoonfuls of the zucchini mixture into the pan. Pat down with a spatula and fry until brown on each side. Repeat with the remaining oil and batter. For the sauce, mix the yogurt, tomato paste and lemon juice together. Serve the latkes immediately with a dollop of sauce on the side.

ZUCCHINI "PASTA" WITH LEMON

2 SERVINGS

I like this dish in the summer, when the zucchinis are deep green and gorgeous and crisp.

1 zucchini
2 Tbsp [30 mL] butter
2 cloves garlic, chopped

It seems that the most essential ingredient of vegetarianism (at least my brand of vegetarianism, which, as I said before, springs from the Italians), is good olive oil, which is not only good for you (it actually dissolves cholesterol), but also tastes good and is much more digestible than butter. The gourmet magazines will insist on extra virgin olive oil, which nine times out of ten is nonsense. Extra virgin (supposedly the first pressing of ripe olives) has become little more than a name for the mass-marketers. The only real extra virgin oil is produced by a very small number of very small estates, and it's so expensive that it's often measured out right at the table with a teaspoon. Real extra virgin olive oil is much too expensive to cook with, and heat can easily destroy its delicate flavour. But a tablespoon or two added to a salad (or beans) will make a dramatic difference—you'll taste the rich freshness of good olives, and, like the Italians, you'll dip your bread in any oil left at the bottom of the dish. You may never want to eat butter again. —*Peasant's Alphabet*

1 sweet red pepper, chopped
Sprig of fresh tarragon or ½ tsp [2 mL] dried
Zest and juice of 1 lemon
½ cup [125 mL] pine nuts, toasted

CUT THE ZUCCHINI into thin pasta-like strips with a vegetable peeler. Melt the butter in a frying pan over medium heat and add the garlic and red pepper. Sauté for 2 minutes. Add the zucchini, tarragon and lemon zest and peel, and cook for 3 minutes more. Sprinkle with pine nuts and serve.

BLACK-EYED PEA CURRY
2 SERVINGS

This curry is delicious when served over rice.

2 Tbsp [30 mL] vegetable oil
1 onion, coarsely chopped
5 to 6 cardamom pods
1 Tbsp [15 mL] curry powder
2 Tbsp [30 mL] chopped tomatoes
1 Tbsp [15 mL] chopped carrot
1 Tbsp [15 mL] chopped sweet red pepper
1 can [14 oz/398 mL] black-eyed peas, rinsed and drained
2 hot red peppers, minced
½ tsp [2 mL] salt
Chopped cilantro

HEAT THE OIL a large frying pan over medium heat. Add the onion and cardamom pods and sauté until the onion is browned. Stir in the curry powder, tomato, carrot and sweet red pepper. Add the peas to the pan along with 1 can of water. Bring to a boil, reduce the heat and simmer the mixture, covered, for 5 minutes. Add the hot red pepper and salt, and simmer for another 5 minutes. Serve with cilantro.

SPICY CHICKPEAS WITH TOMATOES AND LIME
2 SERVINGS

2 Tbsp [30 mL] vegetable oil
2 tomatoes, chopped
1 clove garlic, chopped
1 small onion, chopped
2 small green chili peppers, chopped
½-inch [1 cm] piece fresh ginger, chopped
1 can [14 oz/398 mL] chickpeas, rinsed and drained
Juice of 2 limes
Salt and pepper
Handful of cilantro, chopped

HEAT THE OIL in a saucepan over medium-high heat. Add the tomato, garlic and onion, and cook, stirring, for 3 to 4 minutes, until the tomato starts to collapse. Add the chili peppers and ginger, and cook for another 2 minutes. Stir in the chickpeas and lime juice, and cook for 3 minutes. Season with salt and pepper. Serve with cilantro sprinkled over top.

Chickpeas are the cheapest protein you can buy. Cook your own and they'll have a crunch. (They're no trouble, just put them to soak in water before you go to bed or work. To cook them on the stovetop, drain well, add lots of fresh water, bring to a boil, then turn the heat down to simmer for at least 45 minutes. Or just rinse and leave them all day in a slowcooker on low—fill one-third of the well with beans and cover with water to ½ inch of the top.) If you insist on buying canned ones, drain them, rinse them well to get rid of the slimies, and serve them as if they were real food. Once you discover dried chickpeas you'll discover all kinds of recipes because people will bring them to you as special gifts. Chickpea people have passwords and a secret handshake. There's a spring in their step, a confidence radiating from their smile. Could it be simply their inner works reacting to the extra protein they're getting? Or is it something more? —*Flash in the Pan*

Recollections of

RICK AND SONIA TAKHAR

OWNERS, ASHIANA TANDOORI RESTAURANT, VANCOUVER, BC

James Barber, the great Vancouver legend on the food scene, accomplished so much—from writing books to hosting TV shows. He worked very hard to make Vancouver famous in the food world. His cooking inspired us and we created a mushroom recipe, Mushroom Corn Methi Malai, that he loved.

James loved good food. We met him in 1983 when we opened our restaurant Ashiana Tandoori. He wrote *Best Eating in Vancouver* in 1985, and his quotes in the book about Ashiana Tandoori made us very popular.

James lives on and left a great impression on many people's lives. We are indebted to him forever. We wish he were here to celebrate Ashiana's twenty-fifth anniversary with us. We will miss James always and he will remain in our hearts forever.

ASHIANA TANDOORI RESTAURANT'S MUSHROOM CORN METHI MALAI

Rick and Sonia Takhar

Serve this curry with rice or naan.

2 Tbsp [30 mL] vegetable oil
2 tsp [10 mL] garlic, minced extra-fine
2 tsp [10 mL] ginger, minced extra-fine
1 tsp [5 mL] cumin seeds
½ cup [125 mL] coconut milk
½ cup [125 mL] whipping cream
½ cup [125 mL] fresh or frozen corn kernels
2 Tbsp [30 mL] tomato paste
Pinch of salt
¼ cup [50 mL] cashew butter
¼ cup [50 mL] dried, unsweetened ground coconut
2 Tbsp [30 mL] ground fenugreek
1 Tbsp [15 mL] coriander
Chilies (adjust quantity to preferred spiciness)
¼ tsp [1 mL] white pepper
½ lb [250 g] fresh mushrooms

HEAT THE OIL in a medium saucepan over medium heat. Add the garlic paste, ginger paste and cumin seeds, and cook until light brown. Stir in the coconut milk, cream, corn, tomato paste and salt, reduce the heat and simmer for 5 minutes. Stir in the cashew paste, ground coconut, fenugreek, coriander, chillies and pepper, and then add the mushrooms. Cover and simmer for 5 minutes, or until the fat separates from the curry. Let stand for 10 minutes before serving.

LAYERED TORTILLA PIE

2 Tbsp [30 mL] vegetable oil
2 chilies, chopped
2 cloves garlic, chopped
2 tomatoes, chopped
1 green pepper, chopped
1 onion, chopped
1 tsp [5 mL] cumin
1 pkg 9-inch [23 cm] flour tortillas (6 or 8)
1 can [14 oz/398 mL] refried beans
2 cups [500 mL] shredded cheddar or
    Monterey Jack cheese
1 can [14 oz/398 mL] corn kernels, drained
Handful of cilantro, chopped

PREHEAT OVEN TO 375F [190C]. Heat the oil in a frying pan over high heat. Add the chilies, garlic, tomato, green pepper, onion and cumin, and cook for 5 to 6 minutes. Place a tortilla in the bottom of a round 9-inch [23 cm] casserole dish or springform pan. Top with a layer of the tomato mixture, a layer of beans and ½ cup [125 mL] of the cheese. Top with another tortilla and repeat layering as above, inserting a layer of corn and cilantro. Repeat layering with the remaining ingredients, reserving a little of the cheese. Top with a tortilla and sprinkle with the remaining cheese. Cover with foil, leaving some space above the cheese, and bake for 20 to 30 minutes. Remove from the oven, let stand for 5 minutes, slice into wedges and serve.

VIETNAMESE LETTUCE WRAPS

Serve these wraps with a bit of soy sauce on the side for dipping.

2 Tbsp [30 mL] vegetable oil
1 pkg [500 g] firm tofu, crumbled or
    shredded
2 green onions, chopped
1 carrot, grated
1 tomato, chopped
½ sweet red or green pepper, chopped
1 tsp [5 mL] cumin
Sprig of basil, chopped, or 1 tsp [5 mL] dried
Dash of sesame oil
Dash of soy sauce
Iceberg lettuce leaves, washed and dried

HEAT THE VEGETABLE OIL in a large frying pan or wok over high heat. Add the tofu, green onion, carrot, tomato, red pepper, cumin and basil, and cook for 2 to 3 minutes. Remove from heat and toss the mixture well with the sesame oil and soy sauce. Spoon some of the tofu mixture onto a lettuce leaf and roll it up. Repeat with the remaining filling. Serve.

The Genius of James Barber

DRESSINGS, SAUCES & CONDIMENTS

It's not all that complicated; you don't need a two-hundred-dollar Cuisinart, or a twenty-speed blender, not even a fancy French whip to free yourself forever from the bondage of the bottled salad dressings. Put the stuff in, screw the lid on unless you want your friends to lick the dressing off you and shake it well. That's all. (You can use the same technique for blending flour or cornstarch and water to thicken a sauce.) Just shake it well, stick your finger in to taste it, and fix it up the way your tongue tells you to, remembering never to put it on green salads until just before you're going to eat. That way the greens stay fresh. —*Fear Of Frying*

BASIC VINAIGRETTE
MAKES ABOUT ¾ CUP [175 ML]

You can add almost anything to this vinaigrette— grated cheese, orange juice, garlic, an egg or sherry.

- ½ cup [125 mL] oil (olive, sesame, walnut, hazelnut or grapeseed)
- 2 Tbsp [30 mL] Dijon mustard
- 2 Tbsp [30 mL] vinegar or juice of ½ lemon
- 1 tsp [5 mL] dried herbs (try thyme, rosemary or tarragon) or sesame seeds, crushed
- Pinch of sugar
- Salt and pepper

PLACE THE OIL, mustard, vinegar and herbs in a jar, toss in a little sugar, salt and pepper, screw the lid on tight and shake well.

TERIYAKI SAUCE
MAKES ¼ CUP [50 ML]

Fry bite-sized pieces of fish (e.g., salmon or halibut), chicken or meatballs in this sauce until golden brown and caramelized, about 5 minutes. Serve garnished with green onion.

- 2 Tbsp [30 mL] vegetable oil
- 1 Tbsp [15 mL] soy sauce
- 1 tsp [5 mL] sugar
- ½ tsp [2 mL] cayenne pepper (optional)

HEAT A FRYING PAN over medium heat and pour in the oil. Then pour the soy sauce into the middle of the pool of oil. Add the sugar and cayenne (if using) in the middle of this and stir.

PAPAYA DRESSING
MAKES 1 CUP [250 ML]

The seeds of the papaya give this dressing a good peppery flavour. Good on fruit or green salads, this dressing can also be used as a marinade for meats. Refrigerated, it keeps for one week.

- ½ papaya
- 1 Tbsp [15 mL] sherry
- 1 Tbsp [15 mL] vegetable oil
- Juice of ½ lemon
- Pinch of salt

SCOOP THE FLESH and seeds out of the papaya half and place them in a food processor or blender with the sherry, vegetable oil, lemon juice and some salt. Blend until smooth.

FLOWER AND HERB VINEGAR

Lovely, lovely gifts.

FILL A CLEAN JAR with sprigs of rosemary, juniper berries, chili peppers and pink peppercorns. Fill the jar with white wine vinegar, leaving ½ inch [1 cm] headroom. Seal and leave on a sunny windowsill for three weeks. Strain, reserving the liquid. Arrange some fresh herbs or flowers attractively in a jar and fill with the flavoured vinegar. Use thyme, lavender, oregano, nasturtiums, chive flowers, marigolds, lovage, borage, roses or any combinations you like.

My favourite all-purpose spice is ginger. I use it with chicken, fish and stir-fried vegetables (asparagus, eggplant, cabbage and almost any Chinese vegetable). Poached pears, rhubarb and cooked apples go very well with grated ginger, as do pork chops and tofu and thinly sliced beef. I called my first cookbook *Ginger Tea Makes Friends*, after an Indonesian friend showed me how to make a lovely, comforting tea from fresh ginger and honey. Ever since, I've found ginger as necessary to my cooking as garlic. Even the smallest corner store seems to sell it these days. The trick is to buy it fresh and plump, with the skin all shiny, and use it before it dries out. If you have a great big lump, cut it into chunks as big as a wine cork, put them in a jar, which you then fill with sherry, and keep in the fridge. Sherry and ginger are a great taste combination, so any time you need a bit of ginger, just fish out a lump, grate it or chop it, and use it immediately. If you feel a cold coming on, the jar is there for a quick remedy, or, to be more polite, you can put it in a glass and add a little whiskey. —*Cooking For Two*

PICKLED GINGER

PUT SOME PEELED slices of ginger into a bowl. Sprinkle with a little salt and sugar and 1 to 2 tsp [5–10 mL] rice vinegar. Allow to stand for at least 20 minutes and serve as a garnish.

SUPER ALL-PURPOSE PEANUT SAUCE
MAKES ABOUT 2 CUPS [500 ML]

This peanut sauce will keep in the refrigerator for a month and transform almost any food into something really exotic. Thai and Vietnamese cooks add fish sauce to the basic mixture; others add curry paste, but the essential flavour is peanuts, garlic, a little hot and spicy, a little bright with the lemon juice.

Spread this sauce on anything barbecued—hamburgers, small cubes of chicken on sticks, fish, pork chops, tofu, those skinny little Japanese eggplants, grilled tomatoes, corn or fish. Mix it with lightly steamed vegetables (broccoli, green beans, cauliflower, baby squash) or dilute it a bit with water, lemon juice or a little sherry and toss it with salad greens.

4 red chili peppers, chopped, or 1 tsp [5 mL] hot sauce
3 cloves garlic, chopped
1-inch [2.5 cm] piece fresh ginger, finely chopped
1 can [14 oz/398 mL] coconut milk
¼ cup [50 mL] chunky peanut butter
¼ cup [50 mL] water, beer or even Coca-Cola
2 Tbsp [30 mL] brown sugar
2 Tbsp [30 mL] sesame oil
Juice of 1 lemon

PLACE THE CHILI PEPPER, garlic, ginger, coconut milk, peanut butter, water, brown sugar, sesame oil and lemon juice in a food processor or blender, and process until the mixture is smooth. Store, covered, in the refrigerator. The sauce will thicken, but it thins out as it warms up.

BASIC QUICK PEANUT SAUCE
MAKES ABOUT ¼ CUP [50 ML]

A simpler version of the Super All-Purpose Peanut Sauce, this basic, lasts-for-three-days sauce goes with just about anything—chicken, fish, vegetables—or just spread it on bread.

1 heaping Tbsp [20 mL] peanut butter
Juice of 1 lemon
½ tsp [2 mL] red pepper flakes
2 Tbsp [30 mL] beer, water, wine or whiskey

IN A BOWL, mix the peanut butter with the lemon juice and red pepper flakes. As you mix, the sauce will become stiff. Thin it out by stirring in the beer.

Every time I go to France, I take a five-gallon pail of peanut butter. Customs officers wave me through, after raising their eyebrows and their shoulders, then rolling their eyes in that uniquely French way that says, wordlessly and effectively, that there is no point in trying to understand anybody who isn't French. Peanut butter isn't illegal in France, but it certainly isn't *cuisine française*. Despite being enormously popular, it's almost impossible to find in Paris and even harder to come by in the country. My pail is always empty in a couple of days. The Citroëns and the Renaults start to arrive within minutes and people happily trade a couple of bottles of good wine or some expensive *foie gras* for a dollar's worth, which they take home and eat—like 90 percent of North American kids—with bananas in sandwiches. Peanut butter just doesn't seem to turn up as a main ingredient in cookbook indexes. You'll find recipes for peanut sauce that involve tracking down fresh Louisiana peanuts (medium-large) and spending three hours blanching, drying, roasting, skinning and finally grinding them to produce something archly called "the paste," but you won't often find the simple instruction "take 2 heaping Tbsp peanut butter." Which is a shame, because a jar of crunchy peanut butter can turn the simplest ingredients into kid-friendly, visitor-impressing and, most important, quick-and-easy-on-the-cook dishes of the kind that I call "almost gourmet." For example, if you serve peanut butter with a big plate of cut-up vegetables (cauliflower, sweet peppers, carrots, green onions, whatever's fresh and colourful) and chunks of good crusty country bread, or pita or tortilla chips, and you encourage people to be gluttonous, kids will suddenly begin to like vegetables. There are hundreds of other simple recipes that call for peanut butter. Just make sure you buy the best you can, with "100 percent peanuts" on the label. —*One-Pot Wonders*

QUICK BLENDER HOLLANDAISE SAUCE
MAKES 1 CUP [250 ML]

Pour this hollandaise over cooked asparagus or other vegetables.

3 egg yolks
½ cup [125 mL] hot melted butter
Juice of ½ lemon
½ tsp [2 mL] powdered mustard
Salt

IN A BLENDER, blend the egg yolks on high speed until they are pale yellow and frothy. Keep the blender going and quickly pour in the hot melted butter, lemon juice, mustard and some salt. Blend until the sauce has thickened.

AIOLI
MAKES 1 CUP [250 ML]

Serve aioli with simple steamed potatoes garnished with chopped parsley, with fried potatoes, with pasta, with chorizo sausage or with boiled eggs.

3 cloves garlic
1 egg yolk
1 tsp [5 mL] powdered mustard
½ tsp [2 mL] salt
1 cup [250 mL] vegetable oil

BLEND THE GARLIC, egg yolk, mustard and salt in a blender or food processor until well mixed. Slowly add the oil until an emulsion forms.

Asparagus, *very fresh asparagus*, is one of the world's great luxuries. China, Japan, most of Europe and America, North and South, all grow asparagus, and they all associate it with springtime, with all the wonderful things that come at the beginning of a year, bringing with them all those old-fashioned lovelies of words like "fecund" and "burgeoning" and "vernal." Even "pregnant" comes to have a different meaning in the springtime—the buds and the tips of what may well, in a month, be weeds but right now are beginnings with all the urgency and vitality of something brand new, just *growing*.

Those little bundles in the supermarket, skinny for the first month, plump for the next, green on the shaft and royally purple at the tip are our first and best vegetable, each spear a signpost to summer. We should learn to go past the well-travelled route of *sauce hollandaise*, and take some of the lesser-known roads to pleasure and contentment.

You must, of course, choose asparagus carefully—the cut bottoms of the stalks should still be moist and should not have been strangled by an over-enthusiastic elastic band—and each of them should stand as straight and determined as kids in a school concert choir. If it doesn't fill you with joy and admiration, don't buy it. There will be more tomorrow.

First of all, you will want a coffee pot, garage-sale special. Break the stalks where they break easily, about an inch from the bottom, and stand them, points up, in the coffee pot, and cook them lid on, for between 4 and 8 minutes, depending on the size. Pour off the water, take off the lid, and there you have perfectly cooked asparagus, the tops steamed and the bottoms boiled, ready for a sauce of lightly curried yogurt (or melted butter) and immediate consumption. —*Peasant's Alphabet*

AIOLI AMB FRUITA
MAKES ABOUT 2 CUPS [500 ML]

Serve this aioli with chicken, pork, rabbit or chorizo sausage.

1 ripe quince or 2 ripe apples
    or pears or 1 can [14 oz/398 mL] pears
3 to 4 cloves garlic, chopped
½ tsp [2 mL] salt
Chopped parsley
1 avocado, peeled and pitted
Juice of ½ lemon
Pepper
¾ cup [175 mL] olive oil

IF USING FRESH FRUIT, peel, core and cube the fruit. Cook the fruit in water for about 5 minutes, or until it is soft. Drain and cool. Blend the garlic with the salt and parsley in a food processor or blender. Add the avocado, fruit and lemon juice, sprinkle with pepper and blend until smooth. Slowly pour in the oil, processing until the mixture is thick and smooth.

MAYONNAISE VERDE

Mayonnaise Verde is so versatile. Try it on asparagus, chicken or fish or even as a base for salad dressing.

1 cup [250 mL] mayonnaise
½ cup [125 mL] parsley, chopped
¼ cup [50 mL] fresh spinach
1 Tbsp [15 mL] chopped pistachio nuts
Few mint leaves
Salt and pepper

PLACE THE MAYONNAISE, parsley, spinach, pistachios and mint in a food processor or blender, sprinkle with salt and pepper and blend until smooth and creamy.

PESTO

Nothing is simpler than some fresh mushroom caps, with a teaspoon of pesto in each, simmered gently in a covered pan with a little butter. Pesto and mushrooms go together in almost any combination. Most recipes for pesto require fresh basil and pine nuts, both sometimes difficult to find and always expensive. There are alternatives. Asiago cheese is half the price of Parmesan, cilantro a quarter the price of basil and walnuts a lot cheaper than pine nuts.

LIGHT PESTO
MAKES ABOUT 1 CUP [250 ML]

2 cups [500 mL] tightly packed basil leaves
3 cloves garlic
½ cup [125 mL] olive oil
3 Tbsp [45 mL] finely chopped walnuts
1 Tbsp [15 mL] pine nuts
1 tsp [5 mL] salt
½ cup [125 mL] freshly grated Asiago cheese
3 Tbsp [45 mL] ricotta cheese
2 Tbsp [30 mL] butter

IN A FOOD PROCESSOR, blend the basil with the garlic, olive oil, walnuts, pine nuts and salt until the mixture is smooth. (If you intend to freeze the pesto, pack it into jars now and add the cheeses just prior to using it.) Add the Asiago, ricotta and butter, and process until smooth.

WINTER PESTO
MAKES ABOUT ¾ CUP [175 ML]

You can use cilantro instead of basil when making any kind of pesto. This pesto is great on pasta or steamed new potatoes. You can store it in the refrigerator for a couple of weeks.

1 bunch cilantro
3 cloves garlic
3 Tbsp [45 mL] grated Parmesan cheese
2 Tbsp [30 mL] chopped walnuts
3 Tbsp [45 mL] olive or peanut oil

BLEND THE CILANTRO with the garlic, Parmesan and walnuts in a food processor or blender. With the machine running, add the oil and process until the mixture turns into a paste.

SALSA CRUDO
MAKES ABOUT 3 CUPS [750 ML]

Serve this salsa over hot spaghetti, chicken breast, fish fillets or just with tortilla chips.

4 tomatoes, seeded and diced
2 cloves garlic, chopped
¼ cup [50 mL] chopped cilantro or parsley
¼ cup [50 mL] chopped green onion
2 Tbsp [30 mL] olive oil
1 Tbsp [15 mL] chopped basil or oregano
1 tsp [5 mL] chopped jalapeño pepper or hot
   sauce or ½ tsp [2 mL] chili flakes
1 tsp [5 mL] salt
1 tsp [5 mL] sugar
Juice of ½ lime or lemon

IN A BOWL, combine the tomato, garlic, cilantro, green onion, olive oil, basil, jalapeño, salt, sugar and lime juice. Let stand.

STEVE LITTLE

CHEF DE CUISINE, JOE FORTES SEAFOOD AND CHOP HOUSE, VANCOUVER, BC.

Recollections of

Having grown up in Vancouver, I have been lucky to be influenced by the bounty of seafood available, as well as the different cultural cooking styles in the city. I grew up watching local cooking shows like James Barber's *The Urban Peasant*. His unique, friendly style and attitude towards life always made his show a pleasure to watch and made cooking an interesting hobby for me as a child. As a chef I appreciate his straightforward approach to cooking; keeping it simple, fresh, tasty and most of all fun.

Thank you, James, for helping me become the chef I am today.

124

Steve Little

JOE FORTES' CEDAR PLANK SOCKEYE SALMON

Lightly grilled asparagus, roasted organic baby potatoes tossed in olive oil and Carrot Kimpura (page 105) are great accompaniments to this recipe.

> Sockeye salmon fillets, cut into 5- to 7-oz [150–200 g]
>   portions
> Bourbon BBQ Sauce (recipe next page)
> Cedar planks
> Tomato Jam (recipe next page)

MARINATE THE SALMON fillets in Bourbon BBQ Sauce overnight. Soak the cedar planks in water for 1 hour before use. Preheat oven to 375F [190C]. Place the salmon fillets skin-side up on the planks and roast for 5 minutes. Turn the salmon and continue to cook for another 6 to 8 minutes, depending on the thickness of the fish. Fresh sockeye is best prepared medium rare to medium. When the salmon is cooked to the desired doneness, top with the Tomato Jam and serve on the cedar planks for a "wow" presentation.

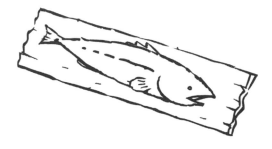

JOE FORTES' BOURBON BBQ SAUCE
MAKES 4 CUPS [1 L]

2 tsp [10 mL] vegetable oil
½ large white onion, diced into medium-sized pieces
½ cup [125 mL] brown sugar
3 Tbsp [45 mL] white vinegar
⅓ cup [75 mL] ketchup
1 tsp [5 mL] Tabasco sauce
½ to 1 tsp [2–5 mL] chili powder
1 oz [25 mL] bourbon

HEAT THE OIL in a saucepan over medium heat and sauté the onion until translucent. Add the brown sugar and stir until dissolved. Pour in the vinegar and continue to cook, stirring occasionally, until the liquid is reduced by half. Add the ketchup, Tabasco and chili powder and bring the mixture to a boil. Reduce the heat to low and simmer for 5 minutes. Stir in the bourbon and cool immediately.

JOE FORTES' TOMATO JAM
MAKES ABOUT ½ CUP [125 ML]

To make the herb sachet, wrap the herbs in a piece of cheesecloth and secure it with kitchen twine.

4 Roma tomatoes, blanched, peeled and diced into
   medium-sized pieces
1 shallot, finely diced
Sachet of fresh thyme, basil and bay leaf
⅓ cup [75 mL] sherry vinegar
⅛ cup [25 mL] sugar
Salt

SAUTÉ THE TOMATO and shallot in a large pan with the sachet until the tomato partially breaks down. Strain the juice from the tomato mixture and set the juice aside. Continue to cook the tomato mixture until all the liquid is gone. Discard the sachet. In another saucepan, combine the reserved tomato juice with the vinegar and sugar, and cook over medium heat until it forms a thick liquid. Combine the tomato mixture with vinegar mixture. Season with salt.

Steve Little

DUXELLES
MAKES ABOUT 1 CUP [250 ML]

When the local market has mushrooms on special, or when you invite forty people to a supper of broiled mushrooms and only two come, when somebody gives you ten pounds of mushrooms ("I found them in the street, I think they fell off a truck"), when you finally and irrevocably decide to give up canned food, cigarettes and Chinese food that arrives in a Volkswagen—whatever the reason, this is a good way to have a few almost-fresh mushrooms on hand for a quick omelet or a frittata, to stiffen up a stew or decorate a fish. Making a lot takes no more time than making a little, so you can double the quantities. Store it in little pots, one in the refrigerator for instant access, the others in the freezer.

1 medium onion, finely chopped
4 Tbsp [60 mL] butter
1 lb [500 g] mushrooms
¼ cup [50 mL] sherry (optional)
1 tsp [5 mL] salt
1 tsp [5 mL] thyme
½ tsp [2 mL] pepper
Big pinch of grated nutmeg
2 to 3 parsley sprigs, very finely chopped

COOK THE ONION in the butter over low heat, covered, until the onion is soft and lightly coloured. (Stir for the first minute of cooking, then cover. This will probably take 15 to 20 minutes; stir again halfway through cooking.) Finely chop the mushrooms, either with a knife or in a blender or food processor. Add mushrooms to the onion, raise the heat to medium and cook, stirring, for about 5 minutes. Add the sherry (if using), salt, thyme, pepper and nutmeg, and stir well. Reduce the heat to low and simmer the mixture for up to 30 minutes, until almost all the juices have evaporated. Stir in the parsley and cook for 2 to 3 minutes. Put the duxelles into little containers and let cool before you cover it.

MUSHROOM BUTTER
MAKES 1 CUP [250 ML]

The British are very big on flavoured butters, because they still have tea. Not just tea as a drink, but tea as a small meal, as an institution, as a special occasion when small talk is made about large issues. North America is not structured around tea; here, we go for chocolate bars and ice cream to bridge the gap between lunch and supper. But one Sunday afternoon you should fire up the toaster, get out the teapot, wake up your nearest and dearest and try tea, with toast and mushroom butter. Very exotic—they eat it all the time at Buckingham Palace.

When Christmas rolls around, buy a nice cup and saucer, fill the cup with mushroom butter, dribble a little melted butter over the top to keep the air out, wrap it all prettily and have your butler deliver it to the recipient of your gift in the Rolls.

Mushroom butter stores well in the freezer.

¼ lb [125 g] mushrooms, coarsely chopped
6 Tbsp [90 mL] butter
4 anchovy fillets
1 tsp [5 mL] capers
½ tsp [2 mL] salt
¼ tsp [1 mL] cayenne pepper
Juice of ¼ lemon

IN A FRYING PAN over medium heat, cook the mushrooms gently in 2 Tbsp [30 mL] of the butter for about 4 minutes. Place the mushrooms with the cooking butter in a blender or food processor, add the remaining butter, anchovies, capers, salt, cayenne and lemon juice, and blend until very smooth.

mmmushrooms

The Genius of James Barber

MUSHROOM TAPENADE
MAKES ABOUT 2 CUPS [500 ML]

In southern France and along the Mediterranean coast from Barcelona to Genoa, the Spaniards, French and Italians each make their own version of tapenade. The essential ingredients are anchovies, capers and chopped black olives, all of which are cheap and plentiful in the region. Tapenade is spread on bread and pizza-style doughs, served a spoonful at a time beside eggs, tossed with pasta as an instant sauce or piled on crackers for the cocktail parties of the non-native population. You can do exactly the same with this version, or toss it with hot spring vegetables or, for an appetizer, brush thin slices of bread with olive oil, toast them in a 375F [190C] oven and pile the tapenade on them. Tapenade will keep in the refrigerator for up to two months.

1 small can anchovy fillets
2 Tbsp [30 mL] olive oil
½ lb [250 g] mushrooms, finely chopped
½ cup [125 mL] black olives, chopped
1 tsp [5 mL] pepper
Juice of ½ lemon
2 Tbsp [30 mL] butter

FRY THE ANCHOVIES in the olive oil over medium heat, using a wooden spoon to mash the anchovies as you stir. Add the mushrooms and stir frequently. The pan will become dry as the oil is absorbed, but then moisture will appear as juices come out of the mushrooms. When this moisture appears, add the olives, pepper and lemon juice, and cook for 5 minutes, or until the juices have almost disappeared. Toss in the butter and cook for 2 minutes. Use the tapenade immediately or, when cool, place it in a jar and refrigerate for later use.

SUPER SAUCE
MAKES ABOUT 2 CUPS [500 ML]

½ cup [125 mL] red wine
1 cup [250 mL] cranberries
1 apple, peeled, cored and sliced
1 pear, peeled, cored and sliced
Zest and juice of ½ orange
Juice of ½ lemon
2 slices ginger, julienned
2 to 3 Tbsp [30–45 mL] brown sugar
½ tsp [2 mL] cayenne pepper
½ tsp [2 mL] pepper
½ tsp [2 mL] salt

HEAT THE WINE in a saucepan over medium heat and toss in the cranberries, apple and pear slices and orange zest. Stir well. Add the orange and lemon juice, ginger, brown sugar, cayenne, pepper and salt, and simmer for 5 to 10 minutes, until the sauce has thickened. Serve hot or cold.

MANGO CHUTNEY
MAKES ABOUT ½ CUP [125 ML]

Use this chutney on breaded cutlets or with any curries or meat dishes you fancy.

1 Tbsp [15 mL] vegetable oil
3 slices ginger, finely chopped
3 whole red chili peppers
1 clove garlic, finely chopped
½ onion, finely chopped
1 Tbsp [15 mL] sugar
1 tsp [5 mL] vinegar
1 mango, peeled, pitted and chopped

HEAT THE OIL in a saucepan over medium-high heat and stir in the ginger, chili peppers, garlic, onion, sugar and vinegar. When the mixture is bubbling, stir in the mango. Cook until thick and syrupy. Serve hot or cold.

RHUBARB RELISH

MAKES ABOUT 1 CUP [250 ML]

A delightful accompaniment to lamb.

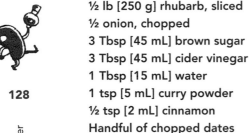

½ lb [250 g] rhubarb, sliced
½ onion, chopped
3 Tbsp [45 mL] brown sugar
3 Tbsp [45 mL] cider vinegar
1 Tbsp [15 mL] water
1 tsp [5 mL] curry powder
½ tsp [2 mL] cinnamon
Handful of chopped dates
Handful of raisins

COMBINE THE RHUBARB, onion, brown sugar, vinegar, water, curry powder, cinnamon, dates and raisin in a saucepan. Bring to a boil and simmer until the rhubarb has softened. Serve hot or cold.

TOMATO, APPLE AND APRICOT CHUTNEY

MAKES ABOUT 3 CUPS [750 ML]

This chutney keeps in the fridge for a month or so and is terrific with curries or simply with some cheese and bread.

I Tbsp [15 mL] vegetable oil
2 cloves garlic, chopped
⅓ cup [75 mL] sugar
¼ cup [50 mL] vinegar
1 tsp [5 mL] cinnamon
½ tsp [2 mL] cloves
Pinch of cayenne pepper
3 tomatoes, chopped
2 apples, peeled and chopped
½ cup [125 mL] dried apricots, chopped
¼ cup [50 mL] water
Salt and pepper

HEAT THE OIL in a saucepan over high heat. Add the garlic, sugar, vinegar, cinnamon, cloves and cayenne, and cook for 2 minutes. Add the tomato, apples, apricots, water and some salt and pepper, reduce the heat to medium and simmer the mixture until the apricots are soft, about 20 minutes. If the mixture becomes too dry, add more water and reduce the heat further.

JUST ENOUGH JAM

My grandmother lived in the same house for 57 years. It was the jam that kept her there. She was good at jam-making and also miserly. The cupboards of her kitchen, the tops of her closets, the basement, even suitcases under the bed were full of jam. Strawberry jam, blackberry jam, marrow and ginger jam, rhubarb jam and even turnip jam. If we were very good, we were allowed to eat it on fresh bread, which she was also very good at making.

Nobody wants an apartment full of jam today, but it is nice, each time a new summer fruit appears fresh in the stores, to make jam once—just enough for a couple of breakfasts or tea with some friends or to have on pancakes.

This way of making jam is foolproof, and it tastes nice, without any of the pectin or other mystery ingredients that usually seem to go into jam-making. Keep this jam in the refrigerator.

1 lb [500 g] hulled strawberries or other summer fruits, not overripe
3 cups [750 mL] berry sugar (use 2 ¼ cups [550 mL] for other fruits)
Juice of 1 lemon

PUT THE STRAWBERRIES, berry sugar and lemon juice in your heaviest saucepan and slowly bring to a boil. Then boil rapidly for 6 minutes, stirring a lot with a wooden spoon. That's it. Put the jam in cups, mugs—anything but teapots.

QUICK BREADS & BAKING

Hollywood used to insist that the West was won with the Colt .45 and the rather convenient habit the Bad Guys had of always wearing Stetsons, which enabled the Good Guys, who were none too bright, to recognize them and hit them over the head with a chair.

But I became convinced at an early age that the real key to survival in cowboy country was bannock, the legendary bread that camp cooks made in th' embers of a dyin' fire and the cowpokes wolfed down with their dawn coffee. For years I tried to make it. I followed all the instructions, I bought hand-milled flour, and once I even carried the water from the "crick" in m'cowboy hat. But nothin' worked. All I got were sodden lumps with a burned outside, too heavy for a Frisbee and too hard for a cushion. I figured that the Code of the West, which came out strong against all sorts of dishonourable behaviour, didn't extend to lyin' about campfire bread. So instead of ridin' off into the sunset, I went Bad and took to kissin' Miss Emmy, even stayin' overnight.

The league of Cowboys for the Code couldn't, by their constitution, gun me down, and I never go into bars that have chairs, so they finally came up with this here recipe and asked me to mend my ways.

It works. The hole is the secret because it lets the heat into the previously soggy middle. It's crusty, it's wonderful with butter, and the only problem is that Miss Emmy likes it so much she reckons I ought to stay every night. —*Flash in the Pan*

BANNOCK
2 SERVINGS

Great fun for kids.

1 cup [250 mL] all-purpose flour
1½ tsp [7 mL] baking powder
1 tsp [5 mL] sugar
½ tsp [2 mL] salt
1 cup [250 mL] milk
1 tsp [5 mL] vegetable oil

MIX THE FLOUR, baking powder, sugar and salt together in a bowl. Add the milk and oil, stirring until a stiff batter forms. Dust your hands with flour and press the batter into a flat cake about ½-inch [1 cm] thick. Poke a hole in the middle (so it looks like a big doughnut). Heat a lightly greased frying pan over high heat for 1 minute and then reduce the heat to low. Place the bannock in the pan, cover and cook for 5 minutes. Turn and cook for 5 more minutes, and then cook 10 minutes more on each side (cook about 35 minutes altogether). Eat immediately with lots of butter and jam or peanut butter.

CORN FRITTERS
2 SERVINGS

1 ear corn
1 onion, chopped
Small piece of spicy sausage, finely chopped,
    or ½ tsp [2 mL] chili pepper flakes
2 eggs
1 Tbsp [15 mL] all-purpose flour
1 tsp [5 mL] baking powder
1 tsp [5 mL] dill
Salt and pepper
1 to 2 Tbsp [15–30 mL] vegetable oil or
    bacon fat

CUT THE CORN kernels off the cob. Put the onion and sausage in the food processor with the eggs, flour, baking powder, dill and some salt and pepper, and mix well. Scrape the mixture into a bowl and stir in the corn kernels. Heat a frying pan over medium-high heat. Form the corn mixture into cakes and fry them in the oil until browned on each side.

My grandmother always asked, "Do you spoon?" when I told her about the most recent of my teenage loves, so I imagine that she, in her time, did it with my grandfather, although any intimate caressing is difficult to imagine since I can't ever recall seeing him without his bowler hat (except when he died and they laid him out on the kitchen table and even then it was on his chest).

But the spooning I remember of my grandmother was another statement of love. She was mean in many ways. I shall never forget her "children's" cocoa, made with cocoa powder and water—no milk, no cream and no sugar. Just a thin mud to drink before going to bed. But in many other ways she was generous—great Yorkshire puddings and, even when I was a six-year-old, "man-sized" slices of beef.

Once a week she made cakes and bread. The kitchen smelt wonderful enough to remember even today, and there were bowls on the table, bowls with cake mix in them and bowls with little bits of dough stuck to the sides. There were also spoons, and these were ours to lick and scour clean with our tongues, while my grandfather, who made his own beer and vinegar, carefully sliced thin the onions he grew and sprinkled them with a little salt, a lot of pepper and his brown malt vinegar.

After the nibbling of the spoons, and the picking out of the dough lumps, there was the waiting while the bread and the cakes baked and the onions marinated. This was the story-telling time, with tales about the lifeboat and the shipwrecks and the pigs he raised to win prizes, and it was the time when my grandmother washed the bowls and the tabletop and of course the spoons, even though they were already licked cleaner than any soap and water could make them.

When the bread came out of the oven, my grandfather cut it immediately, great thick slices for almost-as-thick slabs of cheese, and over the top we spooned the marinated onions. Sometimes in summer we spooned thick cream over strawberries fresh from the garden, and sometimes in winter we spooned brown sugar over our morning porridge, brown sugar and more thick cream. We ate a lot of soup (with spoons), and we learned to get the top off a boiled egg with a spoon. None of this was spooning, not the way my grandmother saw it. But today, years later, whenever I share a spoon in the kitchen, taste somebody else's muffin mix or scrape the jar for the last bit of jam to put on hot biscuits, I feel as if I'm engaging in an act of love. —*Cooking For Two*

GERMAN ONION TART
ONE 9-INCH [23 CM] PIE

¼ lb [125 g] side bacon, cut into small pieces
1 unbaked 9-inch [23 cm] pie shell
1 large onion, sliced
2 eggs
1 cup [250 mL] light cream
½ tsp [2 mL] pepper
Pinch of nutmeg
Pinch of salt

PREHEAT OVEN TO 375F [190C]. Heat a dry frying pan over medium-high heat. Add the bacon to the pan and cook until crisp, about 6 minutes. Remove the bacon from the pan (leaving the fat in the pan) and spread the bacon over the bottom of the pie shell. Add the onion to the pan and reduce the heat to medium. Cook until the onion is soft and caramelized, about 20 minutes. Meanwhile, in a bowl beat the eggs, cream, pepper, nutmeg and salt until well blended. Place the caramelized onions in the pie shell. Pour the egg mixture over top. Bake for 25 to 30 minutes, until the eggs have set. Remove the tart from the oven and let cool for a couple of minutes before slicing and serving.

GOOD OL' SOUTHERN CORN BREAD
ONE 9-INCH [23 CM] SQUARE BREAD

3 eggs
2 Tbsp [30 mL] sugar
2 Tbsp [30 mL] melted butter
½ cup [125 mL] all-purpose flour
1 Tbsp [15 mL] baking powder
½ tsp [2 mL] salt
2 cups [500 mL] cornmeal
1 cup [250 mL] buttermilk or 1 cup [250 mL]
   milk mixed with the juice of 1 lemon

PREHEAT OVEN TO 375F [190C]. Grease a 9-inch
[2.5 L] square baking pan or frying pan. In a large
bowl, whisk the eggs with the sugar. Pour in the
melted butter and stir until the mixture is smooth.
Add the flour, baking powder and salt, stirring until
the flour is just mixed in. Add the cornmeal and
buttermilk, and stir until smooth. Pour the batter into
the pan and bake until golden, about 30 minutes.

QUICK GARLIC AND OLIVE FOCACCIA
ONE 8-INCH [20 CM] ROUND BREAD

*Dip pieces of this wonderful focaccia in olive oil and
balsamic vinegar.*

2 cups [500 mL] all-purpose flour
1 Tbsp [15 mL] baking powder
1 tsp [5 mL] salt
5 to 6 Tbsp [75–90 mL] olive oil
2 cloves garlic, chopped
⅔ to ¾ cup [150–175 mL] water or milk
1 tsp [5 mL] dried rosemary or fresh chopped
Grated Parmesan cheese
Chopped black olives

PREHEAT OVEN TO 400F [200C]. Into a large bowl,
sift the flour, baking powder and salt. Stir in the olive
oil and garlic, pour in the water and stir to make a
dough. Turn it out onto a floured board and knead
gently. Roll out and pat onto an ungreased round
flat pizza pan or baking tray. Poke holes all over the
dough with your fingers. Drizzle a little olive oil on
the dough and sprinkle with the rosemary and some
grated Parmesan. Bake for 12 to 15 minutes. Press
chopped black olives in the indentations on the
focaccia before serving.

SAMOSAS
MAKES 12

*Samosas are spicy Indian street food. Serve them
with Mango Chutney (page 127). You can bake these
samosas or fry them in 3 to 4 Tbsp [45–60 mL] vegetable oil in a large frying pan for about 5 minutes.*

PASTRY
As for Empanadas (page 134)
   or 1 pkg [8 oz/250 g] frozen puff pastry

ROLL OUT THE DOUGH on a floured board and cut
into small squares.

FILLING
1 carrot, cooked and chopped
1 potato, cooked and chopped
½ onion, chopped
⅓ cup [75mL] cooked peas
2 Tbsp [30 mL] chopped cilantro
1 Tbsp [15 mL] grated ginger
1 Tbsp [15 mL] mustard seeds
½ tsp [2 mL] cayenne pepper
½ tsp [2 mL] curry powder

PREHEAT OVEN TO 375F [190C]. In a bowl, combine
the carrot, potato, onion, peas, cilantro, ginger,
mustard seeds, cayenne and curry powder. Place a
little of the filling on each square of dough and fold
it over, sealing the edges, to make small triangles.
Bake them for 10 to 15 minutes, until browned.

POTATO PIZZA

4 SERVINGS

Good, honest peasant fare.

CRUST
¾ cup [175 mL] milk
1 Tbsp [15 mL] vinegar
1 cup [250 mL] all-purpose flour
1 tsp [5 mL] baking soda
1 tsp [5 mL] cream of tartar
1 tsp [5 mL] salt
Olive oil

PREHEAT OVEN TO 475F [240C]. Combine the milk and vinegar in a small bowl and let stand for a few minutes to allow the milk to sour. Sift the flour, baking soda, cream of tartar and salt into another bowl. Add the soured milk to the flour mixture and stir to make a soft dough. Knead lightly on a floured board and form the dough into a ball. Cut the dough in half and roll each half into a circle. Place both on a dry, flour-dusted baking sheet. With your fingers, form a ridge at the edge of each circle of dough and brush it with olive oil.

TOPPING
1 lb [500 g] potatoes
Olive oil
4 cloves garlic, finely chopped
2 Tbsp [30 mL] Parmesan cheese
1 Tbsp [15 mL] chopped rosemary
Salt and pepper

SLICE THE POTATOES wafer-thin and arrange them in overlapping circles over the dough (like a French apple tart). When the dough is completely covered, scatter the garlic over the pizzas, brush them with olive oil and sprinkle the Parmesan, rosemary and some salt and pepper on top. Bake for 20 minutes.

EMPANADAS

MAKES 8

Don't be afraid to make your own pastry. Just remember two things: (1) the more you handle the dough the tougher it becomes, so work quickly and lightly using either your fingertips, a pastry cutter or a food processor; (2) make sure that all your utensils and ingredients are cool. Then just get on with the job and enjoy the process. If you're in a hurry (which many cooks are), use store-bought pastry.

PASTRY
¼ cup [50 mL] butter
1 cup [250 mL] all-purpose flour
1 tsp [5 mL] baking powder
½ tsp [2 mL] salt
1 egg yolk
4 Tbsp [60 mL] ice water

CUBE THE BUTTER and put it into a food processor with the flour, baking powder and salt. Pulse for about 30 seconds, or until the mixture resembles coarse bread crumbs. Add the egg yolk and pulse again. Pour in the ice water one spoonful at a time, processing until the dough forms a ball and comes away from the sides of the bowl.

If working by hand, work the butter with the dry ingredients until the mixture resembles coarse bread crumbs. Mix in the egg yolk, then mix in the water a spoonful at a time until the dough can be formed into a ball. Wrap the dough in waxed paper and chill for 30 to 60 minutes.

FILLING
1 Tbsp [15 mL] olive oil
½ lb [250 g] ground beef
½ onion, finely chopped
¼ cup [50 mL] raisins
1 tsp [5 mL] chili powder
½ tsp [2 mL] dried oregano
½ tsp [2 mL] cayenne pepper
Salt and pepper
1 egg yolk

PREHEAT OVEN TO 375F [190C]. Heat the oil in a medium frying pan over high heat and sauté the meat until browned. Remove any excess fat. Add the onion, raisins, chili powder, oregano, cayenne and some salt and pepper to the frying pan. Stir well and cook for 5 minutes.

Roll out the dough on a floured board and cut it into 8 rounds (use a saucer or something similar to guide your knife).

In a small bowl, beat the egg yolk. Place 1 Tbsp [15 mL] of the filling in the middle of each round of dough. Dampen the edges of the dough with beaten egg and fold the dough over the meat into a half-moon shape, pressing the edges to seal. Prick the pastry with a fork and brush the tops with more of the beaten egg. Bake for 20 minutes.

COCONUT MUFFINS
MAKES 6

Just a hint of coconut.

3 Tbsp [45 mL] grated coconut
1 cup [250 mL] all-purpose flour
1 Tbsp [15 mL] baking powder
3 Tbsp [45 mL] raisins
2 Tbsp [30 mL] butter
2 Tbsp [30 mL] sugar
2 eggs
1 tsp [5 mL] vanilla
Sugar

PREHEAT OVEN TO 350F [180C]. Grease 6 small muffin tins. Soak the coconut in a little hot water for 5 minutes to soften. Drain. Mix the flour, baking powder and raisins together in a bowl. In another bowl, cream the butter, 2 Tbsp [30 mL] sugar and coconut together, and then beat in the eggs and vanilla. Fold the flour mixture into the coconut mixture and spoon into the muffin tins. Dust with a little sugar and bake for 15 minutes.

SAFFRON AND RAISIN CAKE
ONE 9-INCH [23 CM] ROUND CAKE

If you prefer not to use the oven, you can cook this cake in a frying pan. Melt a little butter in the pan, pour in the batter and cook, covered, over low heat for 20 minutes, or until the centre of the cake is firm when touched. Serve with fresh fruit.

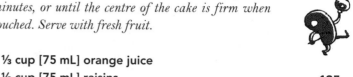

⅓ cup [75 mL] orange juice
⅓ cup [75 mL] raisins
Pinch of saffron
¼ cup [50 mL] butter, softened
½ cup [125 mL] sugar
4 eggs
1 cup [250 mL] all-purpose flour
1 Tbsp [15 mL] baking powder
Pinch of salt

PREHEAT OVEN TO 350F [180C]. Butter a 9-inch [1.5 L] round cake pan. Place the orange juice, raisins and saffron in a small saucepan and heat over medium heat. When the orange juice is about to boil, turn off the heat and let the raisins soak in the mixture until the cake batter is ready.

In a large bowl or food processor, cream together the butter and sugar. Mix in the eggs, one at a time. Add the flour, baking powder and salt, and mix until the batter is smooth. Add the raisin mixture and combine with the batter. Pour the batter into the pan and bake for about 20 to 25 minutes. Allow the cake to cool before serving.

Check your baking powder before starting—drop a little in a glass of water and if it doesn't fizz, it won't work—stir a lot, and make sure you know what your astrological sign is, because carrot cake seems to bring out that kind of thing in people. —*Flash in the Pan*

CURRANT CAKE IN A FRYING PAN
4 SERVINGS

Serve this cake with your favourite tea.

1 egg
⅔ cup [150 mL] milk
1 cup [250 mL] all-purpose flour
1 Tbsp [15 mL] sugar
2 tsp [10 mL] baking powder
Handful of currants or raisins
Zest of 1 lemon
1 Tbsp [15 mL] butter

IN A BOWL, combine the egg, milk, flour and sugar, mixing until the batter is smooth (it should be fairly thin). Let stand for 15 minutes. Stir the baking powder, currants and lemon zest into the batter. Warm a frying pan over low heat and add the butter. When the butter has melted, pour the batter into the frying pan, cover and cook for 10 to 15 minutes, until the top of the batter is just dry. Turn the cake over and cook for 5 more minutes.

CARROT CAKE WITH CREAM CHEESE ICING
ONE 8- BY 4-INCH [20 × 10 CM] LOAF
OR 6 LARGE MUFFINS

An all-time favourite. I sometimes substitute raisins for the pineapple.

CAKE
1 cup [250 mL] all-purpose flour
1 Tbsp [15 mL] baking powder
¼ tsp [1 mL] salt
2 eggs
½ cup [125 mL] vegetable oil
1 can [14 oz/398 mL] crushed pineapple, drained
1 cup [250 mL] grated carrot
½ cup [125 mL] grated coconut
½ cup [125 mL] chopped walnuts
1 tsp [5 mL] cinnamon

PREHEAT OVEN TO 350F [180C]. Grease an 8- by 4-inch [1.5 L] loaf pan or 6 muffin tins. Sift the flour, baking powder and salt into a bowl. In another bowl, beat the eggs with the oil. Stir the egg mixture into the flour mixture. Add the pineapple, carrot, coconut, walnuts and cinnamon, mixing well. Pour the batter into the loaf pan or muffin tins and bake for 25 to 30 minutes, or until a tester inserted in the middle comes out clean. Cool before icing.

ICING
3 Tbsp [45 mL] cream cheese
2 Tbsp [30 mL] butter
1 cup [250 mL] icing sugar, sifted
½ tsp [2 mL] vanilla
Juice of ½ orange or lemon

IN A BOWL, cream the cream cheese with the butter. Add in the icing sugar and mix well. Stir in the vanilla and juice. Spread the icing over the cooled loaf or muffins.

BLACK GINGER CAKE

Have this cake with coffee or ice cream, pack it into lunch boxes or eat it while watching the late movie.

¼ cup [50 mL] vegetable oil
1 egg
½ cup [125 mL] sugar
1 cup [250 mL] molasses
⅔ cup [150 mL] hot strong coffee
2 cups [500 mL] all-purpose flour
¼ cup [50 mL] grated ginger
1 ½ tsp [7 mL] powdered ginger
1 ½ tsp [7 mL] baking powder
1 ½ tsp [7 mL] cinnamon
½ tsp [2 mL] salt

PREHEAT OVEN TO 350F [180C]. Grease a 9-inch [1.5 L] round cake pan. Blend the oil with the egg and sugar, and the stir in the molasses and coffee. Add the flour, grated and powdered ginger, baking powder, cinnamon and salt, and stir until the flour is just combined. Pour the batter into the baking pan and bake for 30 minutes.

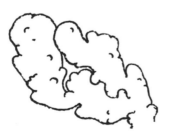

ALMOND PINE-NUT TARTS

These freeze easily. Keep a few on hand for unexpected guests.

¼ cup [50 mL] jam (raspberry is especially
    nice)
12 unbaked 3-inch [7.5 cm] tart shells
2 eggs
½ cup [125 mL] butter
½ cup [125 mL] ground almonds
⅓ cup [75 mL] granulated sugar
½ tsp [2 mL] vanilla
3 Tbsp [45 mL] all-purpose flour
1 tsp [5 mL] baking powder
½ cup [125 mL] pine nuts
Icing sugar

PREHEAT OVEN TO 350F [180C]. Spread a thin layer of jam on the bottom of each tart shell. Place the eggs, butter, almonds, granulated sugar and vanilla in a food processor and process until smooth. Add the flour and baking powder, and process again briefly. Fill the tarts with the almond mixture, and sprinkle a few pine nuts on top of each one. Bake for about 20 minutes. Let the tarts cool. Sprinkle them with icing sugar before serving.

137

Quick Breads & Baking

CARAMEL APPLES ON PUFF PASTRY

2 SERVINGS

1 egg
2 Tbsp [30 mL] milk
½ pkg [8 oz/250 g pkg] frozen puff pastry,
    thawed
1 tsp [5 mL] sugar
2 medium apples
1 Tbsp [15 mL] fresh lemon juice
⅓ cup [75 mL] sugar
¼ cup [50 mL] whipping cream
1 Tbsp [15 mL] Calvados or brandy

PREHEAT OVEN TO 350F [180C]. Grease a baking sheet. In a small bowl, mix the egg with the milk. On a floured surface, roll the pastry into a ¼-inch [5 mm] thick square and brush with the egg wash. Sprinkle 1 tsp [5 mL] sugar on the pastry, and cut it into two triangles. Place them on the baking sheet and bake for 15 minutes, or until golden.

Peel, core and cut each apple into ¼-inch [5 mm] wedges. In a bowl, combine the lemon juice with 1 Tbsp [15 mL] of the remaining sugar and toss in the apple wedges, stirring to coat them with the lemon juice mixture.

Place the remaining sugar in a heavy-bottomed pan over high heat, and cook until it turns medium brown in colour. The caramel will be extremely hot, so be careful not to splash yourself with it. Remove the caramel from the heat, and slowly stir in the cream and Calvados. Toss the apples in this sauce, return the saucepan to medium heat and cook until the apples are soft and the sauce has thickened, about 10 minutes. Serve the warm apples over the pastry.

DESSERTS

You don't have to invite people in for dinner. Let them get it elsewhere. Ask them to come around nine (which is when the real talk starts anyway) for dessert.

They arrive full of their own booze, with food they chose themselves; they're happy (and so are you because you spent two hours in the bath, both of you listening first to a little Brahms, perhaps the Clarinet Quintet, and then the Dvorak Cello Concerto, the Fournier one) and they are anticipatory, because everybody waits for dessert, which is the ideal climate for entertaining. —*Fear Of Frying*

ORANGES WITH TEQUILA
2 SERVINGS

Dessert in a flash.

2 oranges, peeled and sliced
2 Tbsp [30 mL] sugar
¼ cup [50 mL] tequila

LAY THE ORANGE slices in a bowl and sprinkle the sugar over them. Pour the tequila over the slices and let stand for an hour or so.

POACHED PEARS
WITH GINGER AND LEMON
2 SERVINGS

Hot or cold, with or without ice cream.

2 pears, peeled and cored, but left whole
1 cup [250 mL] red wine
½ cup [125 mL] sugar
½-inch [1 cm] piece fresh ginger, grated
Pinch of cinnamon
Zest and juice of 1 lemon

PLACE THE PEARS in a small saucepan. In a bowl, combine the wine, sugar, ginger, cinnamon and lemon zest and juice. Pour the wine mixture over the pears and cook, covered, over medium-low heat for 20 to 25 minutes, turning the pears occasionally. Remove the pears. Boil down the syrup until it is somewhat thick. Serve the pears warm or cold with the syrup.

FROZEN GRAPES
2 SERVINGS

Handful of green seedless grapes
Handful of red seedless grapes
Splash of brandy or sweet wine

PLACE THE GRAPES on a baking sheet lined with waxed paper or paper towels. Put the baking sheet into the freezer, and leave it in there until the grapes are hard (overnight is best). Serve with a little brandy or sweet wine sprinkled over top.

RASPBERRY AND MINT FOOL
2 SERVINGS

They sit and drool over raspberry fool.

2 cups [500 mL] raspberries
Handful of mint leaves
Splash of rum
½ cup [125 mL] whipped cream
Icing sugar

IN A FOOD PROCESSOR, whiz together the raspberries, mint and rum until smooth. Fold in the whipped cream with a fork and sweeten to taste with icing sugar. Serve.

> Plain old vanilla ice cream zipped up with a tablespoon of booze (whiskey, rum, fancy cognac or vintage port, whatever you've got), suddenly becomes a favourite dessert.
> Grating a little chocolate (I've used a frozen Mars bar with considerable success) over a sliced orange is a ridiculously simple one-minute trick to end a dinner. —*Cooking For Two*

BAKED FIGS
2 SERVINGS

6 fresh figs
2 Tbsp [30 mL] honey
Splash of whiskey or rum
Zest and juice of 1 orange

PREHEAT OVEN TO 350F [180C]. Prick the figs with a fork and place them in a baking dish. In a bowl, mix together the honey, whiskey and orange juice. Pour the mixture over the figs. Sprinkle the orange zest over them. Bake for 20 to 25 minutes, or until the figs are soft. Serve warm or at room temperature.

FRESH FIGS WITH RICOTTA
2 SERVINGS

If you can't find fresh figs, use pears or apples or oranges.

6 fresh figs
Icing sugar
1 cup [250 mL] ricotta or cottage cheese
Cinnamon

CUT AN X into the bottom of the figs and gently squeeze them so a bit of the flesh pops out. Roll each fig in icing sugar. Place the figs on a plate, top with dollops of ricotta, sprinkle with cinnamon and serve.

PEARS WITH GORGONZOLA
2 SERVINGS

Straight from God's personal cookbook.

2 pears, cored and thinly sliced
¼ lb [125 g] Gorgonzola or blue cheese, crumbled
Zest and juice of 1 lemon
½ cup [125 mL] almonds, chopped
Sprig of basil, chopped

PREHEAT OVEN TO 400F [200C]. Lay the pear slices on a baking sheet and place a lump of cheese on each. Sprinkle with lemon zest and juice, almonds and basil. Bake for 10 minutes, or until the cheese is melted and nuts are browned.

ROSE PETAL FRUIT SALAD
4 SERVINGS

For very special occasions.

2 kiwis, sliced
2 cups [500 mL] strawberries, sliced
1 cup [250 mL] mango, sliced
½ cup [125 mL] Grand Marnier or orange juice
1 tsp [5 mL] sugar
2 organically grown red roses

MIX TOGETHER THE kiwi, strawberries, mango, Grand Marnier and sugar in a glass bowl and let stand for 30 minutes. Decorate with rose petals.

> Up front. Open. Honest. Bananas Flambé is ridiculously simple, disgustingly rich, gloriously calorific and, because of the ready availability of bananas, habit-forming. Just be a little careful, don't have the heat too high, take them out of the pan with the same care you would offer a day-old baby (anybody who has ever carried a baby about on a spoon will know exactly what I mean) and serve them on warm plates. Don't cook too many at a time: three bananas is enough for the average pan, and besides, it does your guests good to wait for seconds. And thirds. —*Fear Of Frying*

BANANAS FLAMBÉ
2 SERVINGS

These bananas are great with ice cream.

2 Tbsp [30 mL] butter
2 Tbsp [30 mL] brown sugar
Juice of ½ lemon
2 bananas, halved lengthwise
½ tsp [2 mL] powdered ginger or cinnamon
1 oz [25 mL] rum or Scotch

MELT THE BUTTER in a frying pan over medium heat. Add the brown sugar and lemon juice, and stir. Lay the bananas in the pan flat-side down and cook for 3 minutes. Flip the bananas over and sprinkle with ginger. Cook for 2 more minutes and then pour in the rum. Tilt the pan to let the rum catch a flame (this will work only if you have a gas stove; if it's an electric stove, use a match) and flambé! Serve the bananas when the flame has died out.

BARBECUED BANANAS

ALL BANANA DESSERTS are just plain lovely. The simplest of all is barbecued bananas. Lay whole unpeeled bananas on the barbecue over medium heat and cook for 5 minutes. Turn the bananas and cook for 5 more minutes. The skin will go brown. Slide the bananas onto a plate, slit the skin the length of the banana with a sharp knife and open the skin a bit. Put in a knob of butter and some brown sugar, or some yogurt, ice cream or canned milk. Spoon the bananas out of their skins, all buttery and sticky. Eat them right away.

CHOCOLATE FLOWER-COVERED FROZEN BANANAS
4 SERVINGS

2 peeled bananas, cut into chunks
1 Tbsp [15 mL] butter
3 Tbsp [45 mL] cocoa
¼ cup [50 mL] brown sugar
⅛ cup [25 mL] cream
Handful of organically grown edible flower petals (such as lavender, nasturtium, rose or violet)

PUT THE BANANA chunks on a plate, pierce them with toothpicks and freeze for at least 1 hour. Melt the butter with the cocoa, brown sugar and cream in a double boiler or in a microwave, stirring frequently until the sauce is smooth. Dip the frozen bananas into the chocolate sauce and sprinkle with petals before the sauce hardens. Serve immediately.

CHOCOLATE-DIPPED STRAWBERRIES
2 SERVINGS

Bliss!

2 oz [2 squares] semisweet chocolate
2 cups [500 mL] fresh whole strawberries
½ cup [125 mL] whipping cream
1 Tbsp [15 mL] sugar

MELT THE CHOCOLATE in a double boiler. Holding the strawberries by their stems, dip the bottom half of each strawberry into the melted chocolate. Set them on a piece of waxed paper to cool. Whip the cream until soft peaks form, add the sugar and continue to whip the cream until stiff peaks form. Serve the strawberries with the cream.

LEMON CURD
MAKES ABOUT 1 CUP [250 ML]

True love ... in a tart or on toast for breakfast.

5 egg yolks
½ cup [125 mL] sugar
Zest and juice of 2 lemons
2 Tbsp [30 mL] butter

IN A SMALL saucepan over low heat, mix the egg yolks and sugar together, quickly stirring until the sugar is dissolved. Stir in the lemon zest and juice, increase the heat to medium and heat through, stirring constantly until the mixture thickens. Try not to let it boil. Add the butter and stir the mixture until the butter has melted. Remove from the heat and chill until ready for use.

SIMPLE LEMON TART
ONE 9-INCH [23 CM] TART

1 9-inch [23 cm] frozen pie shell, thawed
1 cup [250 mL] Lemon Curd (previous recipe)
Fresh fruit (raspberries and blueberries are great)

PLACE A PIECE of foil in the pie shell and fill it with dried rice or beans (to stop the pastry from puffing up when it bakes). Bake at 375F [190C] for 10 minutes. Remove the foil and beans, and let the pie shell cool to room temperature. Pour the lemon curd into the shell. Chill until just before serving. Cover with fruit and serve.

ROSE CRÊPES
2 SERVINGS

A Valentine's Day natural.

CRÊPES
3 eggs
1 cup [250 mL] milk
6 Tbsp [90 mL] all-purpose flour
Pinch of salt
2 Tbsp [30 mL] melted butter

FILLING
2 cups [500 mL] strawberries, half sliced and
    half partially crushed
Handful of organically grown rose petals
Freshly ground black pepper
Rosewater
Icing sugar

IN A BOWL, mix together the eggs, milk, flour and salt. Let the batter stand for 30 minutes. Meanwhile, in another bowl mix the strawberries with the rose petals and sprinkle with some black pepper and rosewater. Brush a frying pan, over medium heat, with a little butter and pour in 3 Tbsp [45 mL] batter, tilting the pan so that the batter spreads evenly over the pan. Flip the crêpe over and cook for about 20 seconds, until lightly browned. Stuff each crêpe with the strawberry mixture and dust with icing sugar. Serve.

ZABAGLIONE
2 SERVINGS

Just the most sensuous dessert in the world.

4 egg yolks
2 Tbsp [30 mL] sugar
2 oz [50 mL] Madeira, Marsala or sherry

HEAT SOME WATER in a small saucepan to just below the boiling point. Beat the egg yolks in a bowl until fluffy, and then beat in the sugar and booze. Set the bowl over the hot water (make sure the water doesn't boil), and beat the egg mixture for 6 to 8 minutes, until it thickens. Pour the zabaglione into tall glasses and eat immediately, or refrigerate and serve very, very cold.

> Zabaglione is the only dessert that anyone needs to know. It is the best food in the world for two; sensual, easy, rich, mildly intoxicating and so nice that no matter what you have done with the rest of the dinner it will be forgiven and forgotten. The making is foolproof if you take care of two things. It is nice to get the egg whites and yolks separated, but it doesn't matter if you are a bit sloppy. It is nice to use fresh eggs that haven't been in the refrigerator, but it doesn't matter that much. It is nice to use Marsala, but sherry is okay and so is Madeira. I know people who have developed a taste for it with whiskey but none of these things really matters. What is important is to keep beating it and not to use boiling water.
> —*Ginger Tea Makes Friends*

PUMPKIN PUDDING
2 SERVINGS

Serve the pudding with whipped cream or crème fraîche.

2 eggs
¾ cup [175 mL] canned puréed pumpkin
¾ cup [175 mL] whipping cream
2 Tbsp [30 mL] sugar
½ tsp [2 mL] cinnamon
A pinch of nutmeg

PREHEAT OVEN TO 325F [160C]. Grease two small baking dishes. In a large bowl, whisk the eggs with the pumpkin, cream, sugar, cinnamon and some nutmeg until smooth. Pour the mixture into the baking dishes, place them in a baking pan and pour enough hot water into the pan to reach halfway up the sides of the dishes. Bake, uncovered, for 40 to 45 minutes, until the pudding feels firm when touched. Cool to room temperature. Serve.

CHOCOLATE BREAD AND BUTTER PUDDING
4 SERVINGS

8 thick slices white bread, preferably dried
3 Tbsp [45 mL] butter, softened
3 eggs
2 cups [500 mL] milk
2 Tbsp [30 mL] sugar
4 oz [4 squares] chocolate, cut into chunks
Butter

Desserts

PREHEAT OVEN TO 375F [190C]. Butter the pieces of bread and place them buttered-side down in a baking dish. In a bowl, beat the eggs with the milk and sugar. Pour the egg mixture over the bread. Scatter chocolate chunks over the top. Dot with a little butter and bake for 30 minutes, until the pudding is browned and set.

> You can be a convicted dope dealer, a politician, a mugger of the elderly or a stealer of babies' rattles, a stockbroker, wire tapper, hangman, bank manager, even a baseball umpire—but if you can make a decent pudding, you're acceptable in any society.
> —*Flash in the Pan*

PORTUGUESE RICE PUDDING (THE BEST RICE PUDDING IN THE WORLD)
2 SERVINGS

This works only with arborio rice.

2 cups [500 mL] milk
3 Tbsp [45 mL] arborio rice
3 Tbsp [45 mL] butter
3 Tbsp [45 mL] sugar
Zest of 1 orange, chopped
1 tsp [5 mL] cinnamon

PREHEAT THE OVEN to 250F [120C]. Grease a baking dish. Mix the milk, rice, butter, sugar and orange zest together in a bowl and pour the mixture into the baking dish. Bake for 2 hours. Sprinkle with cinnamon and serve hot or cold.

HAZELNUT AND CHOCOLATE SEMIFREDDO
4 SERVINGS

Ice cream without an ice cream maker.

2 cups [500 mL] whipped cream
½ cup [125 mL] hazelnuts, chopped
¼ cup [50 mL] sugar
2 oz [50 g] chocolate, grated
2 egg whites
⅓ cup [75 mL] icing sugar
Splash of rum

PLACE THE WHIPPED CREAM in a bowl and fold the hazelnuts, sugar and chocolate into it. Beat the egg whites until stiff and then fold them into the hazelnut mixture. Gently fold in the the icing sugar and rum. Pour the mixture into dessert glasses or bowls and place in the freezer for 30 minutes, or freeze until set.

FRUIT CLAFOUTI
4 SERVINGS

A French sort of upside-down cake, cooked in a pot, which uses any fruit in season.

3 eggs
1 cup [250 mL] all-purpose flour
1 cup [250 mL] milk
2 Tbsp [30 mL] sugar
2 cans [each 14 oz/398 mL] cherries (or any other fruit), drained
Sugar or whipped cream

PREHEAT OVEN TO 350F [180C]. Grease a baking dish. Beat the eggs in a large bowl with the flour, milk and sugar to make a smooth batter. Put the cherries into the baking dish and pour the batter over top of them. Bake for 30 minutes, or until the batter is puffed up and baked through. Serve sprinkled with a little more sugar or with a dollop of whipped cream.

FRENCH APPLE CUSTARD
ONE 9-INCH [23 CM] ROUND CAKE

Soft-textured apples such as McIntosh or Golden Delicious work well in this cake. Serve it with whipped cream or crème fraîche.

4 medium apples, peeled, cored and thinly sliced
½ cup [125 mL] butter
¾ cup [175 mL] sugar
3 eggs
1 tsp [5 mL] vanilla
Zest of 1 lemon
2 cups [500 mL] milk
1 ½ cups [375 mL] all-purpose flour

PREHEAT OVEN TO 375F [190C]. Melt the butter and grease a 9-inch [1.5 L] round cake pan with some of it. Dust the bottom and sides of the greased pan with some of the sugar. In a large mixing bowl, cream together the butter and all but 1 Tbsp [15 mL] of the remaining sugar until smooth. Beat in the eggs, vanilla and lemon zest, and then stir in the milk and flour. Lay most of the apple slices in the bottom of the baking pan. Pour the batter over the apple slices. Arrange the rest of the apple slices on top and sprinkle with the remaining sugar. Bake for about 1 hour, or until the cake has puffed up and the edges start pulling away from the sides of the pan. Serve warm—the cake will sink once removed from the oven.

DRINKS

Ginger Tea, 149
Homemade Ginger Beer, 149
Ginger Lemonade, 149
Watermelon Juice, 149
Chocolate con Leche, 149
Orange Vodka, 150
Good Queen Bess Mulled Wine, 150
Vij's Chai (Indian Tea), 152
Vij's Yogurt and Tamarind Marinated Grilled Chicken, 153

GINGER TEA

This needs friends and a candle is nice, too, and a good dinner first is great and wine is always wine.

FOR EACH PERSON: a mugful of water, an inch or so of fresh ginger grated coarsely into the saucepan, 2 heaped teaspoons [10 mL] brown sugar (or a bit more honey) and half a lemon (peel and all). Boil (lid on) for 10 to 15 minutes. Strain—just hold back the shreds with something—into mugs and drink as hot as you can.

HOMEMADE GINGER BEER
4 SERVINGS

3 cups [750 mL] ginger tea (cooled)
1 cup [250 mL] club soda or 7-Up

MIX THE SODA with the tea, pour over ice and serve.

GINGER LEMONADE
4 SERVINGS

VARIATIONS: For strawberry lemonade, add 1 cup [250 mL] puréed strawberries with the lemon juice.

3 lemons, whole
3 inches [7.5 cm] fresh ginger, chopped
⅓ cup [75 mL] honey
2 cups [500 mL] boiling water
1 cup [250 mL] cold water

SIMMER THE LEMONS, ginger and honey in the boiling water for 10 to 15 minutes. Remove the lemons and let them cool a bit. Cut them in half and squeeze the juice into the hot water mixture. Pour it through a fine strainer, add the cold water and serve over ice with lemon slices.

WATERMELON JUICE
4 SERVINGS

Terrific on hot days.

4 cups [1 L] small chunks watermelon
2 Tbsp [30 mL] sugar
Juice of 1 lime
Handful of ice cubes

PLACE THE WATERMELON, sugar, lime juice and ice cubes in a blender and whiz until smooth.

CHOCOLATE CON LECHE
4 SERVINGS

If you like hot chocolate, you'll like this.

½ cup [125 mL] boiling water
2 oz [57 g] chocolate (baking chocolate or regular is fine)
4 cups [1 L] hot milk
⅓ cup [75 mL] sugar
1 tsp [5 mL] vanilla
½ tsp [2 mL] cinnamon
½ tsp [2 mL] nutmeg
Cinnamon sticks

POUR THE WATER into a pan and melt the chocolate in it. Add the hot milk, sugar and vanilla, and stir in the cinnamon and nutmeg. Whisk well until frothy and pour into mugs. Put a cinnamon stick in each mug and serve.

Recollections of

SUSAN SAUNDERCOOK
NEWMARKET, ONTARIO

I used to watch James every afternoon—either because I was skipping classes or I was waiting for my shift to begin. I was in university. I was a messy girl in mismatched clothes who played in bands. I never, ever raised a finger in the kitchen and I ordered in a lot of takeout. What I'm trying to get at here: I was the least likely person to watch a cooking show. But this wasn't a regular cooking show. This was a glimpse into James' soul. It was magical.

I wanted to be one of the pesky neighbours who knocked on James' door just as the pot of goodies he was simmering boiled over and got the stove all sticky. I loved that he didn't have neat little bowls of pre-diced, pre-chopped ingredients. He got messy. His kitchen got messy. And he didn't let a little sizzling or smoking get in the way of a good story. I remember extolling the virtues of his show to my friends: "He injects oranges with booze!"

James shared his passion for life through his cooking. And he brought a lot joy into the world. I will miss him.

ORANGE VODKA

The ultimate surreptitious drink!

1 orange per person
Vodka
Syringe

INJECT EACH ORANGE with vodka and suck out the juices!

GOOD QUEEN BESS MULLED WINE
8 SERVINGS

3 cups [750 mL] red wine
1 cup [250 mL] port
½ cup [125 mL] cognac
6 cloves
Pinch of cinnamon
Pinch of nutmeg
Zest of 1 lemon

COMBINE THE WINE, port, cognac, cloves, cinnamon, nutmeg and lemon zest in a saucepan over medium heat and heat until steaming. Do not boil. Serve immediately.

Recollections of

VIKRAM VIJ

COOKBOOK AUTHOR, EXECUTIVE CHEF AND OWNER, VIJ'S, VANCOUVER, BC

When I first opened my restaurant up on Granville Street, I had spent every last penny of my savings and borrowed money from my dad, so it was very critical for me to make every customer happy. One day this old man with a British accent and a beard walks into my restaurant. One of my aversions was to old British men and women telling me about Indian food. "I was born and brought up in India on Indian food," they would boast, as if to say that they knew more about curry than I did. Those kinds of comments used to really offend me, so when this old English gentleman came into my restaurant, my guard was already up. Anyway, he sat down, looked at the menu and ordered a few things. I went over and very politely kept doing the quality check. He seemed to be enjoying it and asked me all these questions about what was in the sauce. Now, I had been making these sauces fresh and not from a can or a jar—even the yogurt was made in the restaurant—so I was particularly sensitive. Anyway, we had a chat about the food, and I had no idea who this person was and why he was asking me all these questions.

When he left, he said a simple thank-you. I thought he did not like my food, and then I saw him talking to somebody outside my restaurant who was about to come in. I started to think that he was telling the person not to come in and I got angry. I was about to go out and attack him because I thought he was bad-mouthing my food. Somehow I did not. A few days later he gave me a very positive review in his article, and I have not looked back since; but if I had hit him, I would not be here, because the guy he was talking to outside was the editor of the *Georgia Straight* at the time.

151

Vikram Vij

VIJ'S CHAI
(INDIAN TEA)

You don't need all of the spices listed below to make chai. At home, we often use just green cardamom, and lots of it! Measure the water and milk using the teacup in which you will serve the tea. Depending on the strength of tea you prefer, use 4 teabags for a milder flavour and 5 for a stronger one. Adjust the sugar according to your preference. Once the chai has cooled, it cannot be reheated.

4 green cardamom pods
5 ½ teacups water
1-inch [2.5 cm] cinnamon stick
1 ½ tsp [7 mL] fennel seeds
About 2 Tbsp [30 mL] sugar
4 to 5 orange pekoe teabags
¾ to 1 teacup whole milk

BREAK OPEN THE CARDAMOM pods. Place the water, cardamom, cinnamon stick, fennel seeds and sugar in a saucepan over high heat and bring to a boil. Add the teabags and boil for 1 minute. Pour in the milk, bring the mixture almost to a boil and remove immediately from the heat. Discard the teabags. Pour the tea through a strainer into a teapot or directly into teacups. Serve while piping hot.

Vikram Vij

VIJ'S YOGURT AND TAMARIND
MARINATED GRILLED CHICKEN

Coconut Rice (page 100) is a nice complement to this dish. Tamarind paste is available at most Asian grocery stores. If the paste has the texture of a fruit smoothie rather than a thick jam, use 2 Tbsp [30mL].

Vikram Vij

¾ cup [150 mL] plain yogurt
¼ cup [50 mL] canola oil
3 Tbsp [45 mL] finely chopped garlic
1 Tbsp [15 mL] tamarind paste
4 tsp [20 mL] salt
1 ¼ tsp [6 mL] cayenne pepper
1 Tbsp [15 mL] garam masala or ground cumin
2 ¼ lb [625 g] boneless, skinless chicken thighs
1 lemon, cut into 6 wedges (optional)

IN A LARGE MIXING BOWL, combine the yogurt, oil, garlic, tamarind paste, salt, cayenne and garam masala. Add the chicken thighs and mix well. Make sure chicken is well covered with the marinade. Cover the bowl with plastic wrap and refrigerate for at least 4 hours and up to 8 hours. The longer the chicken marinates, the stronger the flavours will be.

Preheat a grill, barbecue or stovetop cast-iron grill to high heat. Remember to turn on your exhaust fan if you are grilling on your stovetop, since the cooking process will emit some smoke. Grill the chicken thighs on one side for about 2 minutes, and then turn over. Grill the other side for 2 minutes and turn over again. Grill each side again for 2 minutes, for a total of 4 minutes per side. Poke the thighs with a knife to be sure they are cooked through. If the meat is still pink, grill each side for 1 minute more. Garnish with lemon wedges and serve.

UNLIKELIES

For some readers unfamiliar with the adventurous, irreverent style of James Barber, this book may have already prompted questions like "Lamb with peanut butter, really?" But Barber's friends and fans will not be surprised—they know that in addition to being a tireless cheerleader for anchovies and an evangelical cabbage booster, Barber would gleefully include booze, bananas and peanut butter in recipes where no booze, bananas or peanut butter has gone before. *The Genius of James Barber* would be incomplete without the category of "Unlikelies." Without this chapter, where would a dish like Pasta with Raspberry Sauce go? Is it a dessert? A breakfast? James would not get hung up by such a triviality; he would probably just say, in that unmistakable, gravelly voice, "Try it! You might just like it!"

EGGS IN BEER

1 SERVING

If there are green eggs 'n' ham, let there be eggs 'n' beer!

1 bottle beer or ale
Pinch salt
1 egg
1 slice toast
Paprika
Chopped parsley

IN A MEDIUM SAUCEPAN, heat the beer and salt until simmering and stir the liquid into a whirlpool. Break the egg into a saucer and gently tip the egg into the liquid. Poach the egg for 2 to 3 minutes. Remove the egg with a perforated ladle and place on the toast. Sprinkle with paprika and chopped parsley.

BANANA AND BACON ROLLS

2 SERVINGS

2 bananas, peeled and cut in half crosswise
2 slices bacon, cut in half crosswise
2 slices bread, fried or toasted

WRAP A PIECE of bacon around each banana half. Fasten with toothpicks and broil for 8 to 10 minutes. Serve on the bread.

PASTA WITH RASPBERRY SAUCE

2 SERVINGS

⅓ cup [75 mL] sherry
4 Tbsp [60 mL] raspberry jam
1 Tbsp [15 mL] butter
½ tsp [2 mL] pepper
Juice of ½ lemon
About 2 cups [500 mL] cold cooked pasta
1 orange, sliced

HEAT THE SHERRY, jam, butter, pepper and lemon juice in a pan and, when the mixture is just boiling, pour it over the pasta. Garnish with orange slices and serve.

BANANAS WITH CHEESE AND BRAZIL NUTS

4 SERVINGS

This is really very tasty.

½ cup [125 mL] Brazil nuts
1 Tbsp [15 mL] butter
3 bananas, peeled and sliced lengthwise
4 Tbsp [60 mL] shredded cheddar cheese or
    grated Parmesan cheese
2 Tbsp [30 mL] brown sugar
¼ tsp [1 mL] salt
2 eggs, beaten
½ cup [125 mL] cream
1 tsp [5 mL] cinnamon
¼ tsp [1 mL] nutmeg
½ tsp [2 mL] cayenne pepper

CHOP AND TOAST the Brazil nuts. Melt the butter in a frying pan, lay the bananas in the pan and sprinkle with 3 Tbsp [45 mL] of the cheese and the brown sugar, salt and nuts. In a small bowl, beat together the eggs, cream, cinnamon and nutmeg. Pour the egg mixture over the nut mixture in the pan. Sprinkle with the remaining cheese and the cayenne. Cover and cook slowly over medium heat until set, about 10 to 15 minutes. Serve immediately.

PERUVIAN NOODLE EGGS

2 SERVINGS

Serve these "noodles" on a pool of tomato sauce and sprinkle with grated Parmesan.

4 eggs
3 Tbsp [45 mL] grated Parmesan cheese
3 Tbsp [45 mL] milk
2 Tbsp [30 mL] crushed saltine crackers
Chopped basil
Salt and pepper
2 Tbsp [30 mL] butter

WHISK THE EGGS with the Parmesan, milk, crackers and some basil, salt and pepper. Melt 1 Tbsp [15 mL] of the butter in a frying pan, put in 2 Tbsp [30 mL] of the egg mixture and tip the pan to spread the mixture. Turn the omelette over when done and cook the other side. Remove to a plate and repeat until you have a few. Roll the omelettes up one by one and cut into noodles about ¼-inch [5 mm] wide. When all the noodles are ready, toss them in the frying pan over low heat with the remaining butter and more basil. Serve.

DEVILS ON HORSEBACK

WRAP A PRUNE in a piece of bacon and poke 2 toothpicks through. Fry in a hot pan until the bacon is crisp. Serve as a savoury instead of dessert.

CREAM OF BANANA SOUP

4 SERVINGS

The Scotch bonnet pepper is closely related to the Cuban habanero pepper. They're the hottest in the world. Wear gloves when chopping them.

4 ripe bananas, chopped
1 tsp [5 mL] minced Scotch bonnet pepper
2 cups [500 mL] water
1 cup [250 mL] stock
⅓ cup [75 mL] cream
1 Tbsp [15 mL] rum
Salt and pepper
Sweet red and yellow peppers, julienned, or
    chopped cilantro

PURÉE THE BANANA with the Scotch bonnet pepper in a food processor or blender. Pour the mixture into a saucepan. Heat gently and pour in the water and stock. Cook for 5 minutes. Add the cream and rum, season with salt and pepper and bring the mixture to a boil. Serve hot with the sweet peppers or garnished with cilantro.

TOFFEE WATER CHESTNUTS

6 SERVINGS

An unusual combination. You can use canned water chestnuts if you prefer.

½ lb [250 g] fresh water chestnuts, washed
    and scraped
6 bamboo skewers
1 Tbsp [15 mL] vegetable oil
2 Tbsp [30 mL] hot water
2 Tbsp [30 mL] sugar
2 Tbsp [30 mL] syrup

THREAD THE WATER CHESTNUTS onto the skewers. Heat the oil in a frying pan, add the water, sugar and syrup, and bring the mixture to a boil. Stir until caramelized. Place the skewers in the caramel mixture and turn until the water chestnuts are covered with it. Serve hot or cold.

There comes a time when sitting on the porch spitting watermelon seed interferes with serious conversation. Besides, the seeds pile up after a while, the mailman slips on them and muggers use them for ammunition. But what to do? Every year the watermelons get bigger and cheaper, every year the season gets longer.

Faced with an 18-pound monster, after the second bottle of wine was opened, the obvious became the obvious. Since chicken and watermelon usually come home in the same shopping bag, why not examine their potential for co-existence?

A little rice with it is nice, maybe a couple of fried bananas dusted with cinnamon, or a handful of chopped roasted peanuts. But no matter how you serve it, you have every reason to look smug. —*Flash in the Pan*

CHICKEN WITH WATERMELON
2 SERVINGS

2 chicken breasts, cut into bite-sized pieces
2 Tbsp [30 mL] olive oil
2 to 3 slices fresh ginger, chopped
1 clove garlic, finely chopped
¼ onion, finely chopped
1 cup [250 mL] watermelon peeled,
    seeded and diced
1 tsp [5 mL] curry powder
1 tsp [5 mL] pepper
½ tsp [2 mL] cinnamon
½ tsp [2 mL] salt
1 carrot, slivered or grated

IN A FRYING pan, fry the chicken pieces in hot oil over medium heat. Add the ginger, garlic and onion, and stir well. Toss in the watermelon pieces and the curry powder, pepper, cinnamon and salt. Simmer for 5 to 8 minutes, stirring occasionally. Add the carrot, stir and serve.

LAMB WITH COFFEE
2 SERVINGS

We were doing a show on coffee, and I was racking my brain for one more dish and came up with this somewhat odd combination. A lucky discovery. The slight bitterness from the coffee makes it special.

2 Tbsp [30 mL] vegetable oil
½ lb [250 g] boneless lamb, cubed
6 cloves garlic, chopped
1 onion, chopped
Freshly ground black pepper
2 Tbsp [30 mL] instant coffee
1 Tbsp [15 mL] tomato paste
2 Tbsp [30 mL] vinegar
1 Tbsp [15 mL] brown sugar
1 tsp [5 mL] cumin
3 green onions, chopped
Zest of 1 orange

HEAT THE OIL in a frying pan over high heat and sauté the lamb pieces until lightly browned on both sides. Stir in the garlic, onion and pepper. Add the coffee and tomato paste, and stir well. Add the vinegar, brown sugar and cumin, lower the heat to medium and simmer for 10 minutes. Serve sprinkled with chopped green onion and orange zest.

AVOCADO ICE CREAM
4 SERVINGS

I continue to include a recipe for avocado ice cream in my cookbooks, hoping that one of these days a few of you might try it. You'll either really like it or you won't. I think it's great.

2 avocadoes, mashed
1 cup [250 mL] whipped cream
1 tsp [5 mL] instant coffee
1 tsp [5 mL] lemon juice
1 tsp [5 mL] sugar

MIX TOGETHER the avocado, whipped cream, coffee, lemon juice and sugar. Freeze.

KAREN BARNABY

COOKBOOK AUTHOR, *VANCOUVER SUN* COLUMNIST,
AND EXECUTIVE CHEF, THE FISH HOUSE IN STANLEY PARK, VANCOUVER, BC

160

Karen Barnaby

*M*y first encounter with James Barber was through his book *Ginger Tea Makes Friends*. Twenty-year-olds generally have very little disposable income and I was no exception. What might have been exceptional at the time was what I spent it on. Visiting my local bookstore weekly, I thumbed through the small selection of cookbooks. That activity filled me with a slightly intoxicated feeling as the doors to a whole new world were opened. Every few months a book would come home with me—the special one that I couldn't stop thinking about.

Two that had really captured my imagination were *The Vegetarian Epicure, Book Two*, by Anna Thomas, and *Ginger Tea Makes Friends*, by James Barber. Every week I would go back and forth between the two, agonizing over which one would eventually hold the prized place in my little collection.

I'm embarrassed to say that *The Vegetarian Epicure* won out, only because I was a vegetarian at the time.

Time passed and the recipes from *The Vegetarian Epicure* were forgotten, but the phrase "Ginger Tea Makes Friends" stayed with me like a mantra. Why was that phrase so powerful? Of course, it popped up every time I made ginger tea, but sometimes it would float through my head, not tied to any particular activity or other thoughts.

I always regretted not buying *Ginger Tea Makes Friends* and finally picked it up at a used bookstore on Vancouver Island, near James's island home. I tucked it on the shelf beside *The Vegetarian Epicure*, closing the wide circle that encompassed almost thirty years.

KAREN BARNABY'S
AVOCADO AND ESPRESSO MOUSSE
6 SERVINGS

*James passed this dessert idea on to me verbally for a dinner we hosted together. He described
the avocado and coffee together in that passionate way he had. I thought it was a little odd at
first, but when I developed the recipe, I loved it. It does make sense, since coffee and avocadoes
share the same soil. Serve this mousse within a few hours of making it so that the avocado is
still green.*

161

Karen Barnaby

2 ripe Haas avocados, peeled and pitted
⅓ cup [75 mL] sugar
1 Tbsp [15 mL] Instant espresso powder
2 tsp [10 mL] pure vanilla extract
4 Tbsp [60 mL] mascarpone cheese
1 ½ cups [375 mL] whipping cream
1 Tbsp [15 mL] cocoa nibs (optional)

IN A FOOD processor or using a hand blender, purée the avocado, sugar, espresso and
vanilla until smooth. Add the mascarpone and process until blended.

In a bowl, whip the cream until medium peaks form. Fold the cream into the avocado
mixture, along with the cocoa nibs (if using). Spoon the mousse into 6 dessert glasses and
chill for at least 1 hour before serving.

INDEX

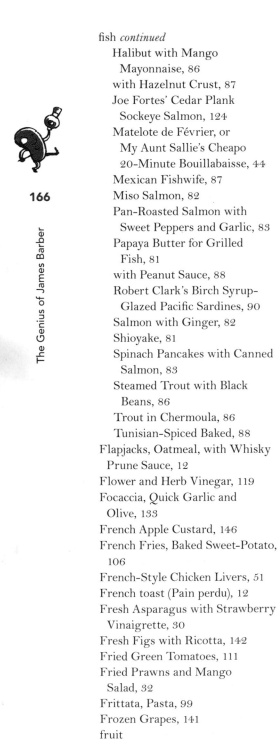